DIE WALKING

DIE WALKING

DIE WALKING

A CHILD'S JOURNEY

THROUGH GENOCIDE

OBADIAH M.

ANANSI

Published in Canada in 2021 and the U.S.A. in 2021 by House of Anansi Press Inc.
www.houseofanansi.com

House of Anansi Press is committed to protecting our natural environment. This
book is made of material from well-managed FSC®-certified forests, recycled
materials, and other controlled sources.

House of Anansi Press is a Global Certified Accessible™ (GCA by Benetech)
publisher. The ebook version of this book meets stringent accessibility standards and
is available to students and readers with print disabilities.

25 24 23 22 21   1 2 3 4 5

Library and Archives Canada Cataloguing in Publication

Title: Die walking : a child's journey through genocide / Obadiah M.
Names: M., Obadiah, author.
Identifiers: Canadiana (print) 20210239026 | Canadiana (ebook) 20210239301 |
ISBN 9781487009724 (softcover) | ISBN 9781487009731 (EPUB)
Subjects: LCSH: M., Obadiah. | LCSH: Rwanda—History—Civil War, 1994—
Personal narratives. | LCSH: Genocide survivors—Rwanda—Biography. | LCSH:
Teenage refugees—Rwanda—Biography. | LCSH: Refugees—Rwanda—Biography.
| LCSH: Teenage refugees—United States—Biography. | LCSH: Refugees—United
States—Biography. | LCGFT: Autobiographies.
Classification: LCC DT450.443.M2 A3 2021 | DDC 967.57104/31092—dc23

Book design: Alysia Shewchuk

*House of Anansi Press respectfully acknowledges that the land on which we operate is
the Traditional Territory of many Nations, including the Anishinabeg, the Wendat, and
the Haudenosaunee. It is also the Treaty Lands of the Mississaugas of the Credit.*

Canada Council
for the Arts
Conseil des Arts
du Canada

ONTARIO ARTS COUNCIL
CONSEIL DES ARTS DE L'ONTARIO
an Ontario government agency
un organisme du gouvernement de l'Ontario

With the participation of the Government of Canada
Avec la participation du gouvernement du Canada

Canadä

*We acknowledge for their financial support of our publishing program the Canada Council
for the Arts, the Ontario Arts Council, and the Government of Canada.*

Printed and bound in Canada

MIX
Paper from
responsible sources
FSC
www.fsc.org   FSC® C103567

FOREWORD

BY GEOFFREY YORK

History is written by the victors. And in the aftermath of one of the last century's greatest tragedies — the horrific wars and mass killings of Africa's Great Lakes region in which millions of innocent people perished — the official histories are still largely told from the perspective of the winner: the long-ruling Rwandan president, Paul Kagame, who rose to power during the genocide of 1994. But the voices of the forgotten are never silenced completely. This book is an extraordinary account of resilience and courage among the Rwandan refugees who suffered innumerable atrocities in the years after the genocide — one of history's most neglected peoples.

Obadiah's story is a child's-eye view of the First Congo War, one of the least-documented conflicts of the twentieth century in one of the poorest corners of the world. It's a story of terror and hunger, massacres and cruelty, during an incredible exodus in which death was so routine that it was scarcely remarked upon, where bodies were simply dragged into the forest and abandoned. But it is also a story of generosity and gentleness among those who endured the worst. It tells us that history is far more complex than the popular stories of rulers and regimes, victors and vanquished, authorized memorials and official myths.

The terrible events of the mid-1990s had their roots in a much earlier refugee exodus. Hundreds of thousands of Tutsis had fled from Rwanda after the anti-Tutsi pogroms that erupted in 1959 and continued through the early 1960s as Hutus won control of the first post-colonial government. The divide between the majority Hutus and the minority Tutsis had been sharpened for decades by the Belgian colonial authorities, who formalized the ethnic differences in ID cards and classroom propaganda. The Belgians had initially propped up a Tutsi elite to rule Rwanda but later switched sides and helped install a Hutu regime in the early 1960s when the country became independent.

The largest number of the Tutsi refugees fled to Uganda, where they joined thousands of Rwandan migrants who had arrived there in earlier decades. By the 1970s and 1980s, cross-border tensions were growing as the exiles dreamed of a return to their homeland. Some gained valuable fighting experience in Uganda's guerrilla wars and as part of the Ugandan army, while the Rwandan government resisted their right of return.

In 1987, exiled activists in Uganda formed the Rwandan Patriotic Front (RPF), a Tutsi-dominated organization that became increasingly militarized, with Paul Kagame its eventual commander. Three years later, thousands of RPF troops crossed the border into northern Rwanda, igniting a war that raged for nearly four years and culminated in the genocide that killed an estimated 800,000 people.

The genocide has often been portrayed, in popular Western accounts, as an episode of pure ethnic hatred somehow unique to Africa—an inexplicable and irrational "tribal" slaughter. But atrocities cannot be understood without their political and military context, and the genocide cannot be separated entirely from the cycles of killing and reprisals that had escalated when the RPF soldiers entered Rwanda.

Relations between Tutsis and Hutus had been increasingly toxic since the early 1960s, exacerbated by exile, dispossession, and the mass killings inflicted on Hutus in neighboring Burundi. The conflict became dramatically more lethal during the RPF military offensive in the early 1990s, as both sides launched violent attacks and used the hate propaganda of their own radio stations to fuel ethnic grievance.

Thousands of young Hutus joined extremist militias. Revenge killings grew worse. And the RPF's brutal tactics during its offensive, including the massacre of Hutu civilians in northern Rwanda, contributed to the atmosphere of fear and paranoia that led to the genocide, in which Hutu militias spearheaded the killing.

The genocide was triggered by the shooting down of a French-crewed jet near the Kigali airport on the night of April 6, 1994. On board the small plane were the presidents of Rwanda and Burundi, who were returning from a summit in Dar es Salaam. The plane was hit by a surface-to-air missile, killing everyone on board.

The plane shootdown is still one of the great mysteries of the twentieth century. But while the Paul Kagame government has always blamed it on Hutu extremists, there is mounting evidence that the missile was fired by Kagame's own RPF forces, eager to sabotage a power-sharing agreement with the government so they could complete their military victory on the ground. Several of Kagame's former aides have given accounts of his role in orchestrating the shootdown. The missile launcher itself has been traced back to the Ugandan military, the main supplier of military hardware to the RPF rebels.

Within hours of the jet's shootdown, Hutu militias launched a brutal slaughter of Tutsi civilians. The orgy of bloodshed continued for three months. The story has been told and retold for decades in books and movies. Neighbour killed neighbour. Bodies were thrown into latrines or mass graves. Hundreds of thousands of Tutsis were murdered: shot at militia roadblocks or hacked to death with machetes. Many who took shelter in churches were massacred with grenades or bulldozed alive inside the buildings. In the first week alone, tens of thousands were killed, and the slaughter continued until July.

At the end of the genocide, after the RPF had captured the country, many Hutus took shelter in temporary camps within Rwanda, but a larger number — a total of about 2.1 million Rwandans — rushed for safety across the border in Tanzania, Burundi, or the Democratic Republic of Congo (known then as Zaire). It was one of the biggest and swiftest exoduses in world history. Many of the refugees were former government officials, Hutu soldiers, and perpetrators of the genocide. But a huge number of them — like Obadiah and his family — were ordinary civilians, including women and children, who had no involvement in the killings.

Many of the camps in Zaire soon became militarized, controlled by soldiers of the former Hutu-dominated regime who mobilized recruits in the camps and trained them for attacks on the new Rwandan regime. They discouraged the refugees from returning to Rwanda. But the refugees' decision to stay in Zaire was understandable: they had genuine reason to fear for their lives if they returned to their homeland. As the RPF seized control of Rwanda in 1994, it was massacring thousands of Hutu civilians across the country. These were not just spontaneous revenge attacks, but highly organized and systematic killings, clearly ordered from above.

In one of the most comprehensive documentations, a team of United Nations researchers led by American consultant Robert Gersony estimated in 1994 that the RPF had killed about 30,000 Hutu civilians in the final two months and immediate aftermath of the genocide. This conclusion was based on a detailed study, including hundreds of interviews across Rwanda.

A common RPF tactics was to visit a village and invite the Hutus to gather for a "peace and reconciliation" meeting. The RPF soldiers, usually drawn from zealous "kill units," would simply open fire and slaughter everyone in the gathering. In another example, in April 1995, thousands of Hutus were massacred by RPF soldiers who had surrounded the Kibeho camp, the largest for internally displaced people in Rwanda. The soldiers killed the Hutus indiscriminately, using machine guns, rocket-propelled grenades, and machetes, while UN peacekeepers watched in horror. Many of the dead were women, children, and other ordinary Hutu civilians. An estimated 4,000 to 8,000 were killed in a single day of carnage.

Finally came the event that Obadiah documents in this book: the Rwandan invasion of Zaire in October 1996, which targeted the Hutu refugee camps. About 800,000 refugees were quickly forced to return to Rwanda. But others refused. Many walked northward, hoping to cross borders to find haven in a neighboring country. They were pursued by Paul Kagame's forces, shooting and killing.

A report by the UN, known as the Mapping Report, was eventually issued in 2010. It documented a systematic pattern: hundreds of deadly attacks on Hutu refugees by the RPF and its Congolese allies in the 1990s killing tens of thousands of Hutus. Most of the victims, it found, were children, women, the elderly, and the sick, "who were often undernourished and posed no threat to the attacking forces." Some of Obadiah's family members were among them.

The UN report raised the possibility that these mass killings could be considered crimes of genocide. It's a question that still haunts Rwanda and Congo today — never properly investigated or answered because of the powerful opposition from Kagame and his allies.

The Democratic Republic of the Congo's famed Nobel Peace Prize laureate, Dr. Denis Mukwege, has repeatedly called for an international tribunal to pursue the findings of the UN Mapping Report and investigate the suspected war criminals who orchestrated the mass killings in Congo. Support for his call has steadily increased for years. Even a quarter-century later, human justice still demands it.

May 2021

GEOFFREY YORK is the *Globe and Mail*'s Africa Bureau Chief, based in Johannesburg, South Africa. He was previously a correspondent in Moscow and Beijing for the *Globe and Mail* and has covered wars in Iraq, Afghanistan, Somalia, Sudan, and Chechnya. He has received a National Magazine Award and five National Newspaper Awards, among other journalistic commendations. Geoffrey is the author of three books, including the national bestseller *The Dispossessed: Life and Death in Native Canada*.

A NOTE ON THE TITLE, AND A DEDICATION

Over the months of April, May, June, and July of 1994, between 500,000 and 800,000 Tutsis and moderate Hutus were murdered in Rwanda. These mass killings are popularly called the Genocide Against the Tutsis. This is an important story to tell and understand, and many have tried, in numerous books, films, and academic articles.

There are other important stories from that time that, while documented, are less well known in the popular imagination. I am speaking in particular about what happened to those — predominantly Hutu — who fled Rwanda during those months and became refugees in neighbouring countries. Many who did so were guilty of genocidal crimes. But the vast majority were just terrified people displaced by horrific violence; I was one of them, a child of fourteen at the time.

I have never talked about what happened to us, but I don't want to be silent anymore. Too much is lost when we are allowed to look at a period of history through one frame only. I want to tell my story because unless we can *all* say what happened to us, unless *all* victims are honoured and memorialized, there will never be real reconciliation or healing in my country.

I dedicate this book to all the victims and all the survivors, to good people everywhere.

This book is a true account. Many of the events portrayed run counter to the official narrative of the Rwandan government, and those who tell similar stories about the period face repression from the authorities. To protect the safety of the author, his loved ones, and other survivors, some identifying details—including the names of certain individuals, places, and organizations—have been changed.

PROLOGUE

* * *

DEPARTMENT OF
HOMELAND SECURITY

CHICAGO, IL

* * *

FEBRUARY 2014

Even though the leg cuffs pained my ankle, I enjoyed walking through the snow. A lot of it had fallen in the night. I didn't like the cold, but I liked the snow very much. Sometimes, driving around with my friend Smith in North Dakota, I would be mesmerized staring out the window at all the falling snow. Hypnotized, I would fall asleep, just like that, in the passenger seat of his car.

I squinted ahead of me and spotted Cabrera further up in the line. I had never seen him as upbeat and confident as he looked that morning. When the buzzer had gone off at 3 a.m., he was already standing with his back against the wall of the cell, twisting the ends of his thick dreadlocks. He had a way of smiling that made his beard seem to vibrate.

The inside of the bus was even colder than outside. There must have been something wrong with the heating system, because the last time I was in that bus I had felt myself cooking like a brochette. Sitting down was a relief for my ankle, though. When I walked, the metal cuff tended to rub up painfully against my ankle bone.

Once we had been on the freeway for a while, a lot of the passengers fell asleep. Their heads bobbed and nodded in unison like the members of a choir. Cabrera was one of them, his dreadlocks bouncing in his lap. I studied the sleeping faces. Some of these guys had been separated from their families for years, most simply because of papers.

Outside, the landscape was only shades of white and black and grey. Snow lay thick on the embankments and capped every bridge and dark, barren tree. If I leaned back and twisted my neck, I could just make out part of the downtown skyline.

I had been to Chicago before. I was amazed by it: the skyscrapers, the roads, the railways — everything so big and so well made. If human beings could build a city as wonderful as this, how beautiful will be the one finally built by God. I told myself again that there is nothing in this life worth holding on to except a cast-iron belief that a better world is still to come.

Homeland Security is housed in a massive brown building in a downtown neighbourhood close to the lake. The lake's water was frozen with the season, and the wind that hit us when we climbed out of the bus brought ice into the bone.

We were body-searched in a narrow room and then, once our shackles had been removed, divided according to our purposes: me, to await my deportation hearing. The room I was taken to was at the end of a corridor in the basement. It was a square, cramped space with fluorescent lights running the length of the ceiling. There were ten or twelve men already waiting, some bent into seats bolted to the wall, others lying on the benches in the middle, trying to sleep. There was a toilet in one corner, and I stood on the opposite side, my back to the wall, as far from the stench as I could get. Strong smells like that always brought to mind memories of the forest.

Sometimes I imagined how this interview might turn out. In those daydreams I would tell them that if they wanted to send me back to Rwanda, they should please just shoot me instead and send my corpse to wherever they thought it belonged. I would tell them I had suffered too much already at the hands of my government. I needed not ever face them again. One day, when she had listened to my story, my daughter would understand.

One

THE GARDEN

We had a vegetable garden next to our house where my mother taught us the rudiments of farming. We lived in the village of Kampi, high in the Rwandan hills bordering Zaire, as the Democratic Republic of the Congo was then named. A region of volcano peaks, lush valleys, and patchwork fields in an array of greens and browns and reds. Maman understood the soil, which was rich but tough to work. She was familiar with the requirements of many different plants.

I liked to work alongside her in the garden, except when it came time to spread the compost she made from food scraps and animal excrement. Then I would hold my nose and protest. She would laugh at me. "You like good stuff to eat, but you don't want to see where it comes from."

My younger brothers and I had to help her with other things too. Chores around the house: sweeping floors, washing dishes and clothes. In our culture, at the time, this was considered "girls' work," but because all four of my parents' children were boys, we had no choice. "You *have* to help me," she said, if we ever complained about it. "You are my sons *and* my daughters."

She had been born to Rwandan parents across the border in Zaire. When she was a teenager her father, my grandfather, had brought the family home to Rwanda so that he could study at the Bible school on the shores of Lake Kivu. Some years after he graduated, my grandparents had gone back to Zaire. They lived there still.

The Christian faith was strong on both sides of my family. My dad's faith was deep and infectious. He had worked as the high school's chaplain for as long as I could remember. A few years earlier, in 1991, he was also appointed as travelling inspector of all schools run by Evangelical churches in the area. For this job, the church had given him a Yamaha AG100 motorbike.

On Tuesdays, he went to Gisenyi, a lakeside town on the border with Zaire. Gisenyi was a major crossing point between the two countries, with lots of goods and people flowing through it every day, and in the evenings he would always return with fresh fish he'd bought in the markets there.

Gisenyi was also home to Maman's younger sister and younger brother, Auntie Peace and Uncle Luc. Luc was only a few years older than me, and if I'd been diligent at school, Papa would let me spend some time there with him and Auntie Peace.

I looked forward to those visits a lot, not least because they had a television set. Luc would borrow VHS tapes from his friends and we would watch movies almost every evening. Chuck Norris was my favourite star. In the first movie of his that I saw, *The Delta Force*, he played a helicopter pilot. After watching that, I began telling people I wanted to be a pilot too.

My little brother Joel, my closest sibling, used to tease me about my ambitions to fly. He said he had heard from a trusted source that Rwandan pilots earned so little they had to steal fuel to make ends meet. Joel was a quiet person, a lot like Maman, but he had a playful sense of humour. He wanted to be a pastor to continue the family tradition.

I didn't know if he was right about the pilots or not. Of the world outside Kampi, I still really knew very little. And not only because we were village kids, although of course that played a role. My parents, and particularly my father, kept the rest of the world out of our home as much as they could. Maybe Papa thought that in this way he could protect us. Though I had uncles in the military, for example, no one even spoke to us about the civil war, which had been raging in Rwanda now for several years. If the subject of the war did come up, Papa simply said our allegiance was to God and to God alone.

So when one of my classmates worried aloud that the civil war would soon reach us, I felt I could reassure him. "My dad will pray and the war will not hurt us."

When I was twelve, our teacher asked all Hutus to raise their hands. In a whisper I asked a friend of mine, who had his hand up, how he knew he was Hutu. He looked at me disapprovingly. "You seriously don't know your tribe? Ask your dad and you'll find out."

Our teacher, who knew my family, told me to raise my hand.

When I asked my father that afternoon, he dismissed the question. I think he wanted me to discover the answer myself once I was old enough to understand.

Sheltered, yes. Naive, certainly. But for years reality had reassured us. War raged but always elsewhere. Most of the time we could forget that anything unusual was going on at all. One Easter, in 1994, this changed for good.

I was on school vacation, and as a reward for achieving good results that term, Papa allowed me to visit Luc and Auntie Peace. That holiday, along with watching movies, Luc and I went to the shores of Lake Kivu every day. We would take off our shoes and watch birds flying over the water.

But then one morning, about a week into my stay, we woke up to the news that the president had been killed in a plane crash and militiamen were everywhere in Gisenyi looking for Tutsis. Already we could hear their war chants in the street outside. I thought with shame how naive I had been, how foolish I must have sounded. My classmates were right: war was here, now.

Militiamen were knocking on every door where they thought Tutsis lived. Each time they came to our compound over the next few days, Auntie's landlord gave them cash so they would not enter. He was Hutu, but his two wives were both Tutsi.

We ventured out of the house only when we had to. We passed the time preparing food and playing cards. Through the windows we could see men in the streets with machetes and axes, chanting for death. It was the most frightened I had ever been in my life.

When we ran out of food after two weeks of being locked inside, Auntie Peace decided it was time to take me back to my parents. We set out for the rural areas on foot early one morning. It was late April. The journey to Kambi, which we could usually make in three hours, took us the whole day as we tried to avoid militia roadblocks. We arrived in my village as the sun was setting behind the mountains.

Two

AKADAPFA

Uncle Rem's Renault was parked outside our house again, his driver sitting inside the cream-coloured car. Over the past three days, my uncle had come and gone and come and gone. He was trying to persuade my father to leave Rwanda, but Papa was having none of it.

It was a week since Auntie Peace had left me with my parents and returned to Gisenyi. We had tried to act like things were normal — Papa went off to work on his motorbike, we prayed and ate together and worked in the garden — but with militias everywhere, it was getting harder and harder to do so.

Uncle Rem, my mother's brother, was a soldier who had been on forced leave since the beginning of the year. His Swahili-inflected accent (he had grown up with Maman in Zaire) had led to suspicions that he was a rebel spy. Also, his wife, Lucie, was from a mixed family; her mother was Tutsi. Rem had witnessed things that year that had made him sick. Sick and terrified.

Another drawn-out conversation took place at the kitchen table. My uncle spoke again about the killings of Tutsis and others, people like his best friend, who was Hutu but had been accused of sympathizing with the rebels and executed. He spoke of the changing tide of the civil war, the likely victory of the Tutsi-led Rwandan Patriotic Front (RPF), and the inevitable time of revenge and retribution to come.

Papa carefully sipped his tea while Rem spoke. Maman listened to her brother intently. I was in the next room with Ebenezer, my brother, who was seven then. Ebe and I were not included in the conversation, but I knew they knew I could hear.

Rem was bald and strong with a large chest. You could see authority in his face. But now he looked tired. He wanted us all to go to Zaire and stay there until the Rwandan future was clearer; my grandpa lived in Zaire's northeast.

My father had a different view. "We have not killed anyone," he said, "so we have nothing to fear." He had said this the day before, and the day before that.

"It makes no difference," Rem said. "Nobody is going to take care to separate who has done what. We need to get out of here as soon as possible."

"No," Papa said. "We have done no wrong. We will stay here as a family with the protection of God."

But there was a loosening in Papa's voice, his words a rope he had been holding on to that he knew he must put down. He was tired too. He buried his head in his hands.

UNCLE REM'S VISIT that day did not end like the previous ones. His presence took on a new shape. Decisions were made, lines were drawn, plans were spoken out loud.

Joel and I would leave with him immediately, travelling to the south to Kibuye and then to a border crossing. Our younger brothers, Ebe and Sy, the four-year-old, would come along with Maman in a few days. We would cross into Zaire together and stay in a refugee camp just across the border until the situation improved. Papa himself had no intention of leaving Rwanda. He hoped things would calm down in a month or so and we would return home.

Only a year and a half apart, Joel and I were used to being paired up. We were also used to taking on responsibility. We went to the room we shared to pack our clothes and a few belongings.

Papa went into his bedroom, and when he came out he was holding the Russian-style winter hat he had bought when he was in Austria for Bible college. It was one of his favourite possessions. He smiled as he fixed the huge white hat onto my head, but I could feel his sadness.

"Pray for us and we will always join you in prayer," he said.

Maman was leaning on the door frame, listening to what we were saying. Even though she trusted her brother, she was not altogether happy with the plan.

I wish we'd known what the end would be. Maybe then we wouldn't have left. Truly, as our culture posits, "Inzira ntibwira umugenzi." *A path cannot tell the traveller what will happen if he follows it.*

Papa and Maman followed us outside. Somehow, in spite of the circumstances, I was excited to climb into Uncle Rem's shiny car. Joel and I had a nickname for it: *Akadapfa,* which means "The Unbreakable." Papa didn't have a car, just the small motorbike.

The inside of Akadapfa smelled of cigarette smoke. My uncle's driver, Moineau, apologized and opened all the windows before he turned the key. *Moineau* is the French word for sparrow. He got the nickname because he could be as talkative as the bird, but what's funny is he looked like a sparrow too, with a slim face and long nose.

Through the rear windshield Joel and I watched as our parents grew distant and then disappeared.

Three

THE ROAD TO KIBUYE

On the road to Kibuye, a narrow dirt lane I had only ever known to be quiet, there was heavy traffic. Cars, trucks, buses, and crowds of people on foot, all going in the same direction. I wondered to myself if everyone had the same plan as us.

We were in the middle of the rainforest of Gishwati when all this traffic came to a near standstill. For hour after hour our car barely moved. Joel and I stared out the window into the thick jungle on either side of the road. "Why don't I see any animals?" I asked. Usually we would see many creatures—monkeys, chimpanzees, birds, and shrews. Uncle Rem laughed. "Do you really think animals want anything to do with this mess?"

A woman was walking alongside our car, tall

and beautiful and wearing a kitenge. With one hand she supported a large bag balancing on her head. She started pleading with us to give her a lift. She repeated the words, "Lift, lift."

Uncle leaned across and told her, "I'm sorry. There's not enough room in here."

A minute later, when she was gone, he said, "Who will feed her? Where will she sleep? If we have to sleep in the car, she can't stay with us, all males. We would have to find her a place. No, no. It will only add problems onto problems." He whispered, defending himself against accusations only he had made.

The afternoon was fast disappearing. At this pace, it seemed unlikely that we would reach Kibuye before nightfall. Frustrated at the logjam, some were abandoning their vehicles on the side of the road to walk. They took with them only things they could easily carry: food, frying pans, blankets. I sensed their fear in the lengthening shadows.

Joel had not said anything for hours; his arms and legs had not moved. He, too, could sense their fear. "Don't worry," I told him. "God can protect us." I didn't yet know from what.

I could not tell how frightened I needed to be. I looked to Uncle Rem's face for answers but couldn't see much there. His teeth were clenched, his eyes looked like a mask's. Moineau was focused on the road ahead.

We continued to move at a snail's pace, slower even than those on foot. I saw the woman in the kitenge alongside us again. Once more she begged us for a ride, but Uncle Rem remained adamant.

A large camp, like a tented town, had sprung up in a clearing in the forest, with people, cars, vans, and trucks stopped all over the place. Some people cooked on small fires near their vehicles. Those who didn't have any food were asking strangers. People looked so tired and scared. I was confused. All I knew was that, in a matter of hours, the world had changed. From that slow-moving car I had seen things I'd never imagined before. A woman giving birth in a huddle of other women. A couple having sex, their bodies pressed together against a tree.

NIGHT HAD LONG since fallen by the time we drove into Kibuye. The city brought no respite, no change of scene or mood. Frightened people searched for safety down every alleyway and on every half-lit street.

We stopped outside a guest house with a wrought-iron gate and flowers in a peeling bed against the wall. Uncle Rem went inside to seek accommodation. Minutes later he returned, disappointed; there were no rooms available here or anywhere else in town. A decision needed to be made. Would we sleep in the car or would we continue driving?

From Uncle Rem's discussion with Moineau, I understood that it would be dangerous to sleep in the car. They decided to buy something to eat and carry on to Kamembe, which was about seventy kilometres to the south. There was a border crossing there.

From a small general dealer, Uncle Rem bought hardboiled eggs and a large Fanta to share. When he got back into the car, he was still laughing at the bloated prices he had paid.

The route to Kamembe was not so busy, and we were able to drive faster than we had all day, which helped us all feel a little calmer. We arrived after midnight, and there we did decide to bed down for a few hours in Akadapfa, parked on the side of the road. Falling into a difficult sleep, I was aware that Moineau stayed up, alert.

WE BREAKFASTED AT a restaurant across the road that opened early. Hungry, I was grateful for the bread and tea, but I found it difficult to concentrate on eating. I overheard people talking about roadblocks, advancing rebels, identification cards. My stomach churned. I was sick with worry for my family left behind, and I had to remind myself of the plan: Maman would follow in a few days with the smaller boys. We would all cross over into Zaire and stay there until things calmed down. Then we would rejoin Papa at home.

"When will Maman come?" I asked my uncle.

"Soon enough," he said. He could see I did not like this answer. Trying to change the mood, he said, "Are you boys ready to go?"

"Go where?" I asked him.

"I don't know. West or south. You pick."

At first, I thought he was joking, but it very soon became clear that, with the outcome of the war uncertain, he really was not sure which direction to take. By asking me, he was throwing the dice. West meant crossing into Zaire, while south would take us to Bugarama, a small town near the borders of Burundi and Zaire, where Moineau's family lived.

The choice for me was easy. I didn't want to cross the border without the rest of the family.

"South," I said.

"South it is."

In Bugarama, Uncle Rem found us a place to stay in another guest house. It even had a restaurant, which was full of people. There was no sign of the war here, at least not to my young mind. We didn't waste any time before sitting down to a hot meal. Brochettes and beer flowed at great speed for my uncle and his driver.

"That's why the innkeepers welcomed us so

warmly," I whispered to my brother. "They'll make a heap of money from these two." For the first time since we left home the day before, I had managed to make Joel smile.

Four

THE BORDER

With the phone lines down across the country, there was no means to communicate long-distance except through informal channels. The best method was to ask people who had come from the same direction. It was a very intricate system, but somehow information was travelling. Two weeks had passed since we'd arrived in town, and there was still no news of Maman and our brothers.

After staying at the guest house for a few days, Moineau's mother invited us to stay at their house. She and Moineau's siblings were courteous to Uncle Rem and they extended that courtesy to Joel and me. They did not have much, but all they had they offered us warmly.

My uncle was eager to get across the border

now. He decided that we should go back to Kamembe to get passports for Joel and me at the immigration office there. No one had thought of organizing passports for us kids before.

I still did not want to cross without my parents. I had a foreboding that if we left Rwanda without them, I would never see them again, but I did not dare worry my uncle with my teenaged premonitions.

It was a shock to see how much Kamembe had changed since the morning we were there, just two weeks earlier. It had been busy then, but now it looked like the end of the world. Confusion reigned in every direction. The streets looked like hospital wards.

Still, we managed to get the passports that same day and returned to Bugarama. People were arriving there too in great numbers, many wounded, some horribly. We heard people talk of the terrible things they had seen: the killing of Tutsis, deaths at the hands of the rebels. I worried about my parents and my brothers.

Days seemed like weeks. Through his military channels, Rem learned that the RPF had taken Kigali, the capital city. He had asked friends of his in the army to help Lucie and their infant son, Noah, get to Gisenyi, but he did not know if they'd made it. It was getting harder for him to cover up his anxiety. Still he tried, and I pretended along with him. But what we attempted to hide was inside every word we said, inside every look.

WE HAD ONCE again returned to Kamembe to see how many people were crossing. When you crossed with lots of others, my uncle explained, there was less risk of being harassed by Zairean officials. We had all our bags with us. Akadapfa was like a moving house.

We needed gasoline, so Moineau drove to a gas station reserved for government vehicles, and that was where Uncle Rem and Moineau saw the white Toyota Hilux parked against a wall. It was empty, but they both immediately recognized it as belonging to a cousin of Rem's and my mom's — Felix, a public servant in those days.

While they were inspecting the number plate, Joel and I saw Uncle Luc coming through the crowd, smiling ear to ear. Behind him was Uncle Felix with his wife, Josephine, and their many kids in tow. And, glory be to God, there was Maman too, leading Sy and Ebe across the lot. When she saw us, Maman sang out and ran towards us. Sy hid behind her, but Ebe left her side and embraced us with Maman.

Standing near the truck, they told us the story of their journey here, of the difficulties they'd had reaching us. Uncle Felix explained how the Interahamwe, the Hutu militia of the ruling party, had wanted to kill Maman. With her lean frame, high cheekbones, and narrow nose, she looked a hundred percent Tutsi, at least in the eyes of these Hutu radicals.

None of them mentioned my father. I did not ask.

The grown-ups talked about crossing the border. There was a comfort in listening to Maman talk about Zaire with Rem. As siblings they had grown up there, so they knew the roads and the languages. For the first time I allowed myself to hope that this trouble would end once we crossed the border. Which, I gathered, we needed to do as soon as possible; RPF troops were advancing countrywide.

Their discussion took an unexpected turn right at the end, when I heard Uncle Rem tell Maman that he had decided to stay behind. She did not question his decision, so how could I? I had to push down my disappointment while Rem and Moineau helped move our things from Akadapfa onto the back of the Hilux.

Uncle Felix was a tall man, dark and slim. He was quite serious-minded but was given to making dry jokes now and then. He gave Joel and me instructions as we looked for space for our bags, and then ourselves, on the back of the truck.

This was the first time we'd been together with our cousins in a big group. The two youngest—Felix's last-born and Sy—sat up in the cabin with Felix and my mom. Felix's other kids and Ebe were on the back in baskets, some of which were stuffed with potatoes. Joel and I sat on a metal roof rack on top of the cabin. Luc hung off the side, holding on to the rack with one hand, his feet on a ledge that jutted out beneath the doors.

"Promise to take care of your mom," Uncle Rem said to me. He was standing next to the truck. "I'll come soon. I need to know what's happened with your dad, right?" I nodded.

The overloaded truck was riding so low the tires were pressed thin. The younger children competed for room with all sorts of household items on the back—a fridge, mattresses, bags of clothes, pots and pans. Joel, Luc, and I held on tight.

The Pont Ruzizi I border post was no more than a kilometre from the gas station, but we immediately found ourselves near the back of a long line of vehicles, all waiting to cross. An hour passed. Then two. We could see the border post and the bridge beyond in the dimming light, but the closer we got, the slower we moved, edging forward only now and then and just a few metres at a time. We crawled like this until at last one of the Congolese officials, seeing that we had Rwandan government plates, waved us on. Uncle Felix swung the Hilux out of the line and accelerated through the gate.

Five

BAKIMBIZI

From up close, the town of Bukavu looked more
developed than Kamembe. I was impressed by the
size of the houses on one side of the road. Impressed
and surprised—I still had a childish fantasy that
everything in my own country was bigger and better
than in Zaire. On the other side of the road was the
water of Lake Kivu, smooth and dark at that late hour.

We were still in the outskirts of the town when
we saw a group of soldiers on either side of the
road ahead of us. Felix slowed right down as we
approached them. One of the soldiers, a long rifle
slung over his shoulder, stepped casually in front
of us and shouted at my uncle, "Get out!" He used
Lingala, a Congolese dialect my mom spoke well
and we all recognized.

We kids had to be helped off the back one by one, all speechless.

Now switching between Swahili and French, the soldiers said they were confiscating all Rwandan government vehicles coming into the country and demanded the keys.

Uncle Felix begged them. He promised he would deliver the car to wherever they wanted the next morning. "Come on. It's nighttime. The kids will be cold and cry." He forced his face into a smile as he looked at us, then back at the soldiers.

When this didn't move them, he pleaded that we needed the car for safety. "We don't know this town. We may be attacked by bandits."

"Why do you take Congolese for thieves?" the first soldier spat.

Uncle Felix realized he had made a mistake; he had offended them and he apologized. But it made no difference. They ordered us to get back into the car and jumped on the pickup's bodywork. Hanging off like bandits—bandits in military uniform—they directed us to a nearby school and there, beside a fence, told us to get out.

There were many people around. Those nearest watched with scant interest as we grabbed our bags and possessions off the truck before the soldiers drove off with it.

Uncle Felix shook his head. What was it I saw in his face? Anger? Shame? It was unpleasant to see this grown man being told what to do like he was a child.

THE JESUIT SCHOOL on the other side of the fence was beautifully painted white. No refugees were allowed inside the grounds.

Refugees: that is how we were already thinking of ourselves. The Swahili word for us was *bakimbizi*, which literally translates as "people running away from something dangerous."

With all the others, we set up camp near the fence with what we had managed to bring—our cooking pots, fridge, bags, a radio set. Many of the things were packed into huge bamboo baskets. It was disorienting to see all these indoor objects out in the open, the ordinary world turned inside out.

That first night was the longest I had ever experienced. Cold and sleepless, except for moments of troubled unconsciousness, we huddled together. Maman and Auntie Josephine shared one mattress, Luc and Felix another. The kids were scattered over the dusty ground.

When dawn finally came and the trees found their form against the lightening sky, I was exceedingly relieved. My brothers and I got up and started looking around for dry sticks so that Maman could light a fire for breakfast. Many more people had arrived in the night. There were *bakimbizi* everywhere, camped as far as the eye could see. In less than a week the town of Bukavu had doubled in population.

FIVE DAYS LATER we were still out there and no longer hoped to find a roof. All around us I could feel a tension between Bukavu's inhabitants and us *bakimbizi*. It seemed to get worse every day. They were worried that we were all *génocidaires* who had come to their country after killing and looting our Tutsi neighbours, and we were worried that they were waiting to prey on our plight, hungry for our remaining possessions.

I wondered how long we were going to have to live like this.

Uncle Felix was sinking into a depression. He hardly spoke anymore, and when he did it was only to make jokes edged with pain. "Now that I have two wives and fourteen kids, I am a truly African man," he sighed.

Maman and Auntie Josephine were not as pessimistic. They spoke good Swahili and could interact with Zairean passersby who stopped to ask the prices of our belongings, assuming that in our desperation we would sell them cheaply. These residents were shocked to hear beautiful Swahili from the mouths of these total *bakimbizi*.

The Jesuit Fathers took good care of the college beyond the fence. I often found myself staring at the long two-storey building. I had no idea when I would be able to return to my own school. I missed my friends, lessons, teachers. I missed Papa too, though I observed an unspoken rule not to ask after him.

We were fortunate, though. Even I, a boy of fourteen, could see that. Many *bakimbizi* had no family left—they had either been killed back in Rwanda or were separated while fleeing. I watched them wandering around, lost: husbands without wives, wives without husbands, parents without children, children without parents. I felt sorry for them.

Old trees lined the streets of Bukavu. Refugees gathered the dried branches and twigs that fell from them for firewood. But we were many, all fighting for the same precious resource. So if we saw two branches on the ground, I would run for one and Joel for the other. On days that we were lucky enough to find four or five suitable sticks, we would return, holding them aloft like trophies, and everyone would congratulate us.

Out searching for wood one afternoon, Joel and

I ventured into a part of Bukavu we didn't yet know. We turned one corner and then another until we could no longer remember where we'd come from. Joel blamed me for not listening to him, since he had warned me on the way that we were getting lost.

It took us almost an hour to find our way back to the big road that led to the school. As we trudged along it, I heard a familiar sound behind us. Our heads snapped around to see a motorcycle approaching from the east with two people aboard. Even from a distance I recognized that bike and the shape of the driver. A shape I would know anywhere on Earth. We sprinted towards it, calling out to our father in one great voice.

Six

THE CLASSROOM

On the back of the bike sat Papa's younger sister. Auntie Abayo was one of my favourite people. Though not that much older than me, she loved me like a son. She was a skilled seamstress who would often mend my clothes or sew me socks as gifts. She was almost Ethiopian in appearance, tall and light-skinned.

Joel and I triumphantly led the two of them to the others, who crowded around to greet them. "God is good," Papa said, getting off the bike.

He explained that so many people had left Kampi that he feared being left alone in the village. I wasn't sure how serious he was. He said he'd had no choice but to join us.

He looked around at the sprawling encampment.

I saw him sniff the air and study the piles of blankets we were calling home. It was a full minute before he said anything. "But we can't live like this," he whispered, to himself as much as to anyone else.

And with that, he left to make connections with pastors of a local church. Papa was not afraid to speak to anyone, and this fearlessness, rooted in his faith, allowed him to make things happen in the world.

Within a few hours of his arrival, we had a better place to live. Our new home was a classroom in a primary school run by the Church of Panzi, about four kilometres away in another part of town. We organized our belongings by family. Each family's were put in a different corner. Our food supplies and cooking equipment were placed together in the centre of the room, since we were all cooking together and sharing meals.

That night, Papa and Auntie Abayo told stories of their journey. Papa recounted how, when they ran out of fuel, they had to push the motorbike for hours because he did not want to leave it behind. If the slope of the road allowed, they would ride it like a bicycle.

We shared with him our own stories. I spoke about the woman I saw giving birth and the woman who kept asking us for a lift. My brothers and I sat close to Papa, protectively. Now that he had come, we wanted to make sure he stayed.

OUR DAD WAS not the only surprising and welcome arrival. The following Sunday morning we
attended the service at the church that the school
belonged to. Before the sermon, the pastor greeted
Papa and asked him to come to the front to intro-
duce the rest of us. This welcoming of visitors is a
tradition in many African churches.

As Papa took the microphone, there came
a commotion from the back of the church and
then the unmistakable voice of Uncle Rem, who
was marching towards the pulpit. My dad almost
dropped the microphone and rushed to hug his
brother-in-law. The whole session seemed to have
been hijacked by our family. Papa collected himself
and introduced everyone, including Rem, and the
service continued.

After church, my uncle explained to us that he
had crossed the border two days before my dad. To
find us, he had waited until Sunday, when he knew
Papa would be praying somewhere, and had bet
correctly on this church. My uncle went outside to
fetch his wife and son, my Auntie Lucie and cousin
Noah. They had fled Rwanda under the protection
of a friend of Rem's, a colonel who was also married
to a Tutsi woman.

Over the next few weeks, more and more of
our family arrived from Rwanda, other uncles and

aunts, until we were thirty people all living in one classroom.

With so many mouths to feed, Maman, Josephine, and Lucie would cook throughout the day. In pots mounted on a charcoal stove they made cassava bread, potatoes, cabbages, and, once in a while, fish with rice. Congolese women moved around selling dried fish, cassava flour, cassava leaves, bread, potatoes, fruits.

During the day we sat outside the classroom, talking or praying, or else looked for firewood. Staying inside was impossible. The roof was made of iron sheets so it got extremely hot.

Nights were an acrobatic challenge to sleep. We shared thin foam mattresses arranged this way and that on the floor. If anyone wanted to change their sleeping position, they had to wake everyone up to turn at the same time.

On moon-bright nights, Luc, Joel, and I played checkers, using a set Luc had brought with him. Sometimes we played until after midnight. It helped get through those nights. Whoever lost surrendered his place at the board.

REFUGEES WERE ALL over the city now, sleeping everywhere like vagrants, relieving themselves on the pavements and in ditches and gutters, wherever they could. The nauseating smell of human excrement was growing strong. And without clean water, people were starting to get sick. Cholera and other diseases stalked the settlement.

Money was running out. Some refugees began to beg on the streets, attracting merciless beatings from local policemen. Others did what they could to survive. In the evenings Luc and Joel and I would sometimes take walks together. On these twilight excursions, women would often approach Luc to ask if he needed sex. They were selling their bodies for as little as two dollars or something to eat.

Another kind of sickness was spreading too: hopelessness, despair. Once, the three of us went out to buy some food on the street. A woman, young, in her early twenties maybe, had climbed up a tall tree. Standing on a branch high above the ground, this woman shouted that she was tired of being alive. Everyone she loved was dead, she said, and she wanted to be dead too.

People tried to persuade her not jump, but we watched as she let herself fall. Luc said I must not go near her body. Red Cross volunteers eventually came and took her away.

It was around this time that I remember having

this strange thought: *This is my situation too. The lives I see around me, this is my life too.*

Even Maman was beginning to lose hope, though she tried not to show it. I watched her suffer in silence. I could see how much she hated to see her children living in these conditions.

One day—we had been in Bukavu for about a month—Uncle Rem decided he had had enough. "We can't live like this," he declared. "Look around. People are dying. We will all die here!"

We were sitting outside the classroom when he said this. The family had just eaten a small meal, now trying to conserve what food we had.

"It makes no sense for us all to stay here. We can give everybody a better chance if some of the older children go to live with Papa." He was referring to his and Maman's father, my grandpa, who lived in the northeast of Zaire.

My parents looked at each other. My mother nodded in agreement. "Let the kids go," she said. "At least they will have food." Emotion trembled in her voice.

The more they spoke, the more it seemed to them the most sensible option. Uncle Luc, who knew the route, would escort Joel and me to Kabalekasha, Grandpa's village.

To me it did not seem a good plan to separate again. Even if things were pretty bad here and getting worse, even if people were getting sick and the nights were uncomfortable, when I was close to my parents the world was in order.

Seven

THE BOAT

Our boat was long and narrow and already over-flowing with passengers. The captain, a heavyset man, explained that we would sail through the night and arrive at the port of Kituku, on Lake Kivu's northern shore, the following morning. From there we planned to catch a lift into the mountains, where Grandpa lived.

Papa and Uncle Rem stood with us on the dock. It was about four days after the discussion outside the classroom. They had come to bid us farewell.

The dock was busy with countless people doing a thousand different things. Selling, buying, loading and unloading boats, all babbling in languages I knew nothing of.

I had never been on a boat before, and I was

nervous because I couldn't swim. When I was eleven, I'd splashed around in a lake with some kids who could. Watching them swim with ease, I'd assumed it was simple and went in too deep. I swallowed gallons of water before they pulled me out. Since then I had been very frightened of water.

Uncle Rem said, "Take care of each other." He had given Luc some money for us to buy food along the way.

"We will pray with you," Papa told us.

I was very emotional back then. I had no option but to turn my face as fast as I could to avoid showing them my weak side.

On deck we found a place for ourselves and our things near the railing. We had with us our bags of clothes, some pairs of shoes, and a foam mattress. I looked around at the other passengers—more than two hundred of them. Many were soldiers of the regime now in collapse back home. I knew that because of their uniforms and the rifles slung around their shoulders. They wore their uniforms crudely, smoked cigarettes, and talked in loud voices.

Besides Rem, I had another uncle in the army: Papa's younger brother, Amos. I had always admired Rem and Amos for their disciplined ways, so to see these soldiers dressed and acting like this was a shock. I recall the smell of their cigarette smoke.

THE BOAT LEFT its mooring and slid out into the lake. I felt a great sense of unease, and I could see that Joel was as scared as I was. The water looked suspicious—in the setting sun, the reddish swells made me feel like we would sink in that blood-like colour.

Darkness fell as the boat sailed slowly north, keeping close to the lake's western shore. We heard people say that this was to escape detection by RPF soldiers who were patrolling the lake on the eastern, Rwandan, side.

I avoided looking at the water sloshing against the side of the boat, and instead fixed my eyes on the dark-blue sky above us, speckled with so many beautiful stars. Below deck a party raged, fuelled by Primus beer and who knows what else. The festivities were loud and raucous.

On deck another kind of pandemonium unfolded. The soldiers tormented the rest of us. "You don't have to worry about falling into RPF hands!" they cried, their eyes shining with strange energies. "If we are attacked, we will shoot everybody first!" It was a joke to them. They laughed and waved their weapons around as they said this, acting out scenes of massacre. Some started to bounce on the side rails, which caused the boat to rock from side to side. People screamed that we would capsize. This just made the soldiers bounce even more, with loud, unhinged laughter. I was cold all over. Joel closed his eyes in fear. Even Luc looked troubled. I longed for the classroom back in Bukavu.

Only a few passengers slept. The rest of us remained awake all night, like people who had taken strong drugs. Dark water surrounded us on all sides. Darkness covered the mountains. I felt in my bones that in no time at all we could become part of forgotten history.

THE BREAK OF day brought more visibility but no relief. The soldiers, lethargic and listless, were less threatening, but now there was more anxious talk among the passengers of RPF patrols on the water close by.

The boat turned towards the western shore and docked at a beach, where we spent the day. Some people went into the nearby communities to buy pineapples and sugar cane. The rest of us stayed on board, eating or trading provisions. The soldiers were in battle gear, prepared to protect the boat — from nothing, as it turned out.

We set off again that evening and sailed all that night under the cover of darkness. This time the soldiers on deck were more watchful. The boat was quieter. Below deck, people still partied, but in a lower key.

Finally, at around 4 a.m., we arrived at the port of Kituku. It was still dark. The dock was crowded with people waiting to unload the boat. We climbed off and exhaled. "Come on," said Luc. "Mugunga isn't far. Let's keep moving."

Eight

IN THE NORTH

Mugunga refugee camp, on the outskirts of Goma, would be a stopover on our way to Grandpa's village. The camp was not far from the port, but to reach it we needed to cross a steep, forested valley.

Many of us from the boat were going to Mugunga. We walked into the trees in close single file so as not to get separated. We carried our belongings on our heads.

The sky was turning from black to grey, but down in the trees it was still mostly dark. All we could see was the back of the person in front of us and dark volcanic soil at our feet. Uncle Luc, carrying the rolled-up mattress, was in front; then Joel, then me behind. To distract ourselves from fatigue, we speculated about our arrival: *Will Grandma recognize us? Who else will be there when we arrive?*

We were walking up the other side of the valley, getting closer to the camp, when I smelled something bad. It was faint at first, but with every step it got stronger. I could see the others were smelling it too. I wished I had something to cover my nose with, but there was no time to open my bag to look for something suitable. I clenched my fist and pressed it to my mouth to stop myself from throwing up.

Then, with a terrible understanding, we saw them. Bodies. Slumped in the undergrowth on either side of the path. Some wrapped in black fabric sheets or loosely tied between mats of wild grass. Some on their own and others piled in twos or threes.

Luc wavered but did not stop. Joel looked back at me. We all continued in silence.

There were hundreds of them — women, men, small children. *Who were they? What had happened here?*

I tried not to look, but my eyes were drawn towards them. This was my first sight of dead bodies. The smell was like spoiled meat, but much worse and stranger. It obliterated thought. We picked up our pace, desperate to get away from there.

MUGUNGA SPRAWLED ON both sides of the tarred road from Goma to Sake for some three to four kilometres, and then another several kilometres from the road to the Nyiragongo Volcano. Only a few refugees had received tents from the local operation of the United Nations High Commissioner for Refugees (UNHCR). Most were living in structures they had fashioned themselves using branches and plastic, or were just out under the sky.

Joel and I stood in one spot while Luc walked around trying to get information on when would be the best time to travel to Grandpa's village. While we waited, I noticed two men pushing a wheelbarrow back the way we had come. In it I saw a human-shaped sack. What we had passed was a burial ground. I tried to turn off the images in my brain.

When Luc came back, he explained that we would need to wait for market day to catch a ride to Shasha, a town close to Grandpa's village. That was three days away.

The camp was so overcrowded that even finding a place to set one's foot was an issue. We walked to the edge of the camp to put our things down. The edges were sought-after: more space, especially space to relieve yourself. Toilets were more than scarce.

The three days passed slowly. We made a pact not to leave one another's sight. Mostly we sat and watched people carrying their dead to the forest. Mugunga — like many other camps in the region — was losing a battle against cholera and other diseases. Every few days bulldozers arrived to bury the bodies beneath the black volcanic soil.

The three of us shared the mattress. Sleep was difficult. The noise was hectic: so many people crammed together, cooking, telling stories of survival. It was impossible to sleep more than thirty minutes before something woke me, either the noise of the camp or a vivid dream of corpses.

ON THE FOURTH morning we headed to the road, where, as Luc's informants had told us, we were soon able to flag down a truck on its way to Shasha. Somehow we managed to find space for our things, and then ourselves, on the crowded bed, just moments before the driver took off at top speed. The more rounds he completed between Goma and Shasha, the more money he made. At any moment, I thought, we are going to tip over and be crushed.

Every time the truck stopped to let people off or on, someone jumped out on the passenger's side of the cabin and jammed a big rock under a tire.

"Welcome to the land of rock brakes," Luc whispered.

Though the trip took less than an hour, we passed

through several checkpoints along the way. Luc warned us to be quiet, lest our accents give away our identity as Rwandans. So Joel and I kept our mouths shut.

Later we learned that Luc's warning to us was wise. Countless other Rwandans travelling to family in the area were killed, especially in Sake, a town between Goma and Shasha, their bodies thrown into the river, food for fish in watery graves. There were many who wanted to discourage refugees from joining their families, who, like our own grandparents, had lived in that area for decades.

At each checkpoint, Luc handed over some of our cash. Anyone who carried a mattress had to pay. Zairean soldiers had not been given their salaries for years, and these bribes from refugees were a new means of survival.

AS SOON AS we jumped off the truck in Shasha, we encountered more trouble. A group of three or four men, calling themselves local leaders, noticed our mattress and demanded that we hand it over along with any money we had. The rule of law had disintegrated. Refugees especially were at the mercy of opportunists like this.

Fortunately, there were many Congolese Rwandophones — speakers of the Kinyarwanda language — living in Shasha, descendants of Rwandans who had fled harsh colonial treatment back in the 1940s, and when some of them noticed what was happening, they formed a shield around us. We ran behind some shops and hid in the dense banana plantation that surrounded the town.

Our defenders soon caught up with us. They explained that our mattress was like gold here, since so many people were destitute, and they advised us to leave it with them and run.

Uncle Luc thanked them for their advice but said he would take his chances with the mattress. An argument ensued, which Joel and I took in like bemused spectators, until at last these Kinyarwanda speakers relented. Then the oldest among them offered more advice. "Go through this valley to Kabalekasha," he said, pointing behind us, into the banana trees. "Forget the path. Just make your way through the trees." I was grateful to them but also wondered whether they were to be trusted. Nothing and no one seemed safe.

Uncle Luc took their advice seriously. Tucking the rolled-up mattress under his arm, he made his way into the grove. Joel and I followed. I thought our attackers would find us no matter which route we took. I saw bodies in the undergrowth, even though there were none there.

Nine

KABALEKASHA

Grandpa in his cool and shaded kitchen gazed at us for a long time before he could say a word. I remembered his face from when I'd last seen him, ten years before: large ears and round, expressive eyes. "We thought you were all dead," he whispered.

They had had no word of us since May, months earlier, and with the news of the killings out of Rwanda, naturally he had feared the worst. "Come closer, my sons. Oh, praise God."

When Grandma and Auntie Peace returned from the market in Shasha (where we must have just missed them), they, too, were overjoyed.

Auntie Peace, whom I had last seen when she left me in Kampi, almost fell over with surprise and then shrieked and wrapped me in a tight embrace.

She had crossed the border and made her way here months ago. Grandma, who had aged more than Grandpa in the last decade, grinned and hummed joyful syllables. She lived in her own world of prayer.

Soon afterwards, neighbours and Grandpa's church members poured into the house to greet us, and relief and happiness spread to the visitors. It was a welcome to remember.

That evening a goat was slaughtered and a feast prepared. All of Kabalekasha's inhabitants — about twenty families — came to greet the pastor's grandchildren. Grandpa watched us eat and stroked his tiny white beard all the while. "Now that I've seen you," he said, "it means I'll see the others too." After the meal, he showed us to our beds. The church had given Grandpa two houses. Their walls, as with every house in Kabalekasha, were made of wood and mud, their roofs grass-thatched. We would stay in the smaller house with our male uncles.

It was very beautiful there in Kabalekasha. In the clear light of the following morning, I could see the villages that populated the surrounding hills. The closest village was Cyigonde, down in the valley, near a glinting stream.

We told Grandpa all about what had happened. How we had fled Rwanda, the separations and reunions, the refugee situation in Bukavu. He listened, serious and attentive. When we explained why Rem and my parents thought we should come here, he nodded in support of their decision.

OUR LIFE IN Kabalekasha soon took on a pleasing routine. Grandpa enrolled us in the church-run school a few minutes' walk from our house, and Joel and I began lessons immediately. Before school, and on most afternoons, Joel and I had to take Grandpa's goats to pasture. On Tuesday and Friday afternoons we went with Auntie Peace to the market in Shasha, where she sold biscuits that she bought in the refugee camps.

We had been here for about a month when, through word of mouth, we received news of the rest of our family. They had left the church compound in Panzi to settle in the refugee camp on the grounds of the Institut National des Études et Recherches Agronomiques (INERA), which gave the camp its name, located about twenty-five kilometres away from Bukavu. The Zairean government had decreed that all refugees must be settled in camps.

I missed them. I wondered how it felt to be living in a refugee camp. But life with Grandpa offered surprising new connections. Joel and I learned that in this region we had lots of family we had never heard about. Some twenty kilometres south of Kabalekasha, in a village called Bitonga, we met my grandfather's sister, who was married to a local Hunde chief. Theirs had been the first intermarriage between a Congolese Hunde chief and a foreigner. We also visited Kavumu, in the mountains further south of Bitonga, where our cousins lived. My grandfather refused to come with us to Kavumu, because it reminded him of his bitter separation from his father when, as a young man, he'd chosen Jesus over traditional African beliefs. He nevertheless didn't mind if we went.

Each place we visited, a goat or sheep was slaughtered in our honour. We ate meat and cassava bread and returned with stories for Grandpa. He would laugh at our tales and recount his youthful time in those mountains, how he had kept his father's cows and how God had decided that he needed to be a shepherd of men, not cattle.

He read to us from the Bible, choosing instructive stories like the one about a certain Samson, who was seduced and betrayed by Delilah. Grandpa wanted us to be disciplined when it came to sex. (He need not have worried; Joel and I were inexperienced and unadventurous in this regard, while Uncle Luc had developed a relationship with a girl he knew from back in Rwanda.)

When we weren't at school or tending to the

goats, we spent our time learning to play guitar. Our teacher was Mundos, the leader of the church's youth choir. We practised joyfully, but we had to take care of the delicate instruments because replacing a broken string, in that part of the world, was not a simple matter. These music lessons were a gift I cherish. Playing the guitar still brings me a peace that surpasses any other.

Ten

UBUNTU

Ubuntu. The term has been popularized in discussions about post-apartheid South Africa, but it is a concept that has its equivalents throughout sub-Saharan Africa. It comes from the Nguni phrase "Ubuntu ngumuntu ngabantu," which means *A person is a person because of other people,* or *We belong, therefore we are* — a sort of African alternative to Descartes's "I think, therefore I am."

It is difficult, without feeling a tragic irony, to even mention *ubuntu* while discussing that period, when hatred along ethnic lines consumed our country and region. But I feel like I witnessed something along the lines of *ubuntu* in North Kivu that year.

The communities where my grandfather pastored consisted of different tribes — Bahunde, Nande,

Havu, Shi, and Banyarwanda, the Kinyarwanda-speaking people — but they all welcomed us as their own. They listened attentively to our stories of how we had fled our country, and brought gifts of food as a sign of solidarity with our suffering.

Some people like to paint Africans before colonialism as demons, some as angels. The truth, of course, is that we were neither. In Kinyarwanda, there is a saying: "Inda ibyara mweru na muhima." *From one womb comes a well-behaved child and a difficult one.* Each society has its own demons, its own angels. However, the sad reality is that the colonists wiped out so much of what was good and strong in our region and exacerbated the weaknesses for their own ends.

In Rwanda it was first the Germans and then the Belgians. Each played into our eventual destruction, as they favoured one group over the other and oppressed the majority with forced and unpaid labour. In fact, originally our "tribes" were just social class distinctions that could change depending on one's economic status. Generally speaking, Tutsis were the cattle herders, the prosperous, and the ruling class — that included the monarchy later overthrown in the independence movement — while Hutus were the farmers, the skilled labourers, house servants, and others considered lower-class.

Cows were a determining factor in status. If you owned eight cows, you were considered a Tutsi: *umutunzi*, wealthy. But that all changed with the mandated identity cards introduced by the Belgians in 1935, which divided us officially and permanently into Hutu and Tutsi, often according to ridiculous, subjective physical features.

And that was that: a deadly cleavage that could be manipulated by those with power and influence. So-called leaders, European and Rwandan, stoked the fires of division, fear, and hatred, and time and time again our country burned itself to the ground.

For a short time, though, in the beautiful hills of North Kivu, I witnessed a different life, a life free of conflict. Being separated from our parents and younger brothers was not ideal, but in that time of upheaval, this was a gentle and nourishing interlude.

WE HAD BEEN in Kabalekasha for a year when this fragile peace—in our own lives, and in that part of Zaire—showed signs of breaking apart. It was mid-1995. I had just turned fifteen. A year had passed since the genocide, and there was now a growing consensus among Zaireans and the international community that Rwandans needed to go back to their country. Insecurity had increased and incidents were blamed on Rwandan refugees. In this area, as throughout Zaire, conflicts flared between, on the one hand, a coalition of the Bahunde and the Nande (two Congolese tribal groups) and, on the other, the Banyarwanda and Rwandan refugees like us.

Some Zaireans started coming for Rwandans' livestock. Before each attack, Grandpa's congregants would come to warn him. In Zaire, back then, it was a taboo to touch a man of God, or even his property, but now, because the attackers would often be people he didn't know, we would have to hide in the banana trees to avoid trouble, sometimes for a whole night.

When such attacks became more and more frequent, Grandpa grew afraid that we would all be killed, and he and Auntie Peace made plans for Joel and me to return to our parents. Luc wanted to stay behind with his girlfriend. He said he would take his chances.

As the representative of the Evangelical community in the refugee camps in Zaire, Tanzania, and Kenya, Papa travelled a lot to assess the needs in all the big camps. This had brought him to Mugunga. When Auntie Peace went to buy her biscuits there, she would visit the Evangelical church to enquire what Papa was up to, and when he would be visiting next. On occasion he had left a letter for us with those pastors, giving news of the family. The next time she went, Auntie learned that he would be in the camp in a matter of weeks. She agreed to take us to meet him then.

It was hard to say goodbye to Grandpa, Luc, Mundos, and all the new family we had discovered. Before we left, we went back for a last visit to each of the extended families, even though it was dangerous as tensions between Hundes and Rwandans grew worse.

But we were also excited, of course — eager to see our parents and brothers and to experience the intricacies of life in a big refugee camp. On the truck back to Mugunga, Joel and I chattered like two birds welcoming sunrise.

Eleven

REUNIONS

We found Papa inside a large blue tent belonging to the church. Our joy was indescribable. He hugged us tightly, and we could feel the love and affection flowing from him to us.

After some discussion between her and Papa, Auntie Peace stayed with us rather than risking a return to Kabalekasha.

We stayed at Mugunga two nights — a Friday and a Saturday — during which time I had a chance to look around. I couldn't believe how many people there were in tents and shelters made of sticks and plastic. The camp was like an endless city sitting low on the ground.

We did not know it then, but Mugunga had grown into the largest refugee camp in the world.

Hundreds of thousands of people from the populous northern Rwandan provinces of Byumba, Gisenyi, and Ruhengeri had taken refuge there.

On Sunday we watched Papa preach his last sermon, and then we set off for Kituku to catch a boat back to Bukavu.

The boat journey was beautiful beyond words, as different from our first crossing a year before as could be. This boat was larger and had decent seats. A light breeze flowed over the water, which remained undisturbed, smooth as glass. When the sun set, water and sky all flowed together and everything glowed burnt red.

There was still much to share about the past year. Papa drank in our stories, smiling and nodding. With a laughing tone he said, "One day I will ask Grandpa if you really were such good kids."

Then he tried to prepare us for what lay ahead. "You have to understand: in the camp you won't be eating many times a day like you did at Grandpa's. You might have only one meal a day."

We told him we didn't care, and honestly it did not matter to me. All I wanted was to be reunited with Maman, Ebe, and Sy.

INERA REFUGEE CAMP was located on the grounds of an agricultural research centre run by the Zairean government, which had given some of its fields to the UNHCR to settle Rwandan refugees. There were now two million of us in Zaire.

A tarred road separated INERA from a series of marshland farms where local Zaireans grew vegetables to sell to refugees. The rows of tents were numerous and so dusty with the ochre-coloured soil that from a distance they looked red. Only when one got closer to the camp was their original white colour visible, with a few light-blue ones here and there.

Papa led us through the tents, turning left and right and forward and back—it seemed like an elaborate maze—until we saw Maman, Auntie Abayo, Ebe, and Sy, who were all waiting for us with open arms. We could not have hoped for a warmer and more joyful arrival. To celebrate, Maman and Auntie Abayo had prepared a big meal of lentils and pâte jaune, or yellow maize paste.

I was amazed at how thriving and organized INERA seemed—so different from the sprawling destitution at Mugunga. Refugees had started small businesses that served not only other camp residents but also the local population. Restaurants selling meat, chapatis, and cassava leaves opened early and closed late—an alternative, for those who could afford it, to the pâte jaune and lentils provided by the World Food Programme (WFP).

New survival skills were needed and rewarded, and in those days reversed many people's fortunes. Some of the rich became poor and some of the poor, rich. Public servants and academics struggled to adapt, whereas hustlers prospered and became the new wealthy class. Some even said they preferred their new life in the camp to the life they had left behind.

It was not as peaceful as it had been in the mountains with Grandpa, but for Joel and me, INERA was bearable, even livable; it was an existence full of games and all sorts of youthful relationships.

Some of these relations worried our father, who was always going off to community meetings to discuss how to curb the drug use, prostitution, and petty crime that was so common in the camp. The thought that we would get swept away in all this vice weighed on him.

"You guys need to be good role models," he would tell us. "Stay away from these things. Concentrate on your studies."

INERA's school — where Joel, Abayo, and I were enrolled — was hardly worthy of the name. It was housed in several large tents in a field about five hundred metres from the edge of the camp's third zone, where we lived. Classes were packed well beyond capacity, with over two hundred students per class, and the teacher would show up maybe once a week. Mostly we would spend our days playing football or volleyball behind the tents.

Papa worried about the school for other reasons too. He knew that among its organizers were people who had taken an active part in the genocide. Some of them had come to his church and confessed their sins. Papa had no power to refer these people to any legal body—none existed in the camp—but he feared their influence on young minds.

We also knew that in the second zone were some powerful people from the old regime, including the former president, Théodore Sindikubwabo. He and others kept a low profile; no one, especially in the other zones, knew much about them.

Some of the refugee camps, especially in the north, were turned into military bases by ex-soldiers of the Forces armées rwandaises (FAR) still loyal to the genocidal regime, but I didn't see anything like this at INERA. While many Hutus had been brainwashed into perceiving a mortal threat posed by all Tutsis—"Kill or be killed" was the propaganda—most refugees I knew hated the militias. And more and more were turning against them as the magnitude of the genocide emerged.

Still, people like Papa, who condemned the genocide openly, attracted enemies. Some accused him of being a spy for the RPF. My father was not troubled by the slander. He busied himself with helping people and finding us another school.

Twelve

INERA

Papa enrolled us in a local school about two kilometres from the camp. I was excited when I heard it was one of the best in the area. This excitement soon waned, however, as we found it difficult to make friends. Our Congolese classmates spoke in *mashi*, a local language, whenever they wanted to gossip about us refugee kids. They wondered why we weren't studying at the camp school. "You're paying double what we pay, yet you have free schools in your camp?" I felt embarrassed and avoided such questions.

When I was not in school, I spent time with Papa at the orphanage he and another pastor had organized in the camp. There, more than three thousand children received food, clothes, and schooling while

Papa and his colleagues worked to reunite them with their parents or else find families to adopt them. Médecins Sans Frontières (MSF) nurses helped with medical care.

I was — and still am — proud of Papa's care for these orphans. I found in his work a helpful perspective. Compared to these kids I was blessed. My family's lives were in limbo for yet another year, but we were all together.

Also, Papa had a plan for us to return home. We would go first to Nairobi and from there make our way back to Rwanda. I wasn't told about this idea directly because it was a difficult, and controversial, decision. Some of the other refugees considered returning a betrayal — a sign of being a sell-out or even a collaborator. I heard they would prevent you from leaving, sometimes going so far as to kill those who tried.

Another concern for Papa was his work. At INERA he had brought together Christians from different churches; his church was flourishing, the orphanage relied on him. He didn't know how to leave his sheep behind.

I thought about home a lot — my friends, my school — and tested my nostalgia against the news that came from Rwanda.

The country was in ruins: bankrupt in every way,

its economy and social fabric torn apart. Even as the new government tried to rebuild the nation after the genocide, people continued to flee—most, as we had, into Zaire. They arrived in INERA with stories of killings still happening against both sides, by those affiliated with the former government and those connected to the new one, as well as vengeance among neighbours.

I turned sixteen in May of 1996. By that time we had been away from home for more than two years. I could feel my limbs lengthening and could see the same in Joel. I did not hear much more about Papa's plan to go home. Even Uncle Rem's old desire to move as far as he could had waned. I think he enjoyed being with his sister and brother-in-law, and Lucie, his wife, was several months pregnant. A kind of inertia had set in.

School at least had become a lot easier since the local kids began to accept our presence. Actually, I was kind of pleased to be returning to class after a long and relatively uneventful break when we heard on the radio that a new war had broken out, and everything changed overnight.

The new Rwandan army had crossed the border, saying they had come to find and destroy Hutu militia hiding here. Zaire was already in chaos, especially its east, burdened by us refugees and torn apart by warlords and ambitious armed factions. The Rwandan forces found an ally in the opposition leader Laurent Kabila, who had cobbled together under his command a coalition of local rebel groups. They called themselves the Alliance des Forces Démocratiques pour la Libération du Congo-Zaïre, or the AFDL. When Burundi, Angola, and Eritrea joined the invasion, the First Congo War—Africa's First World War—began.

Our relatively stable existence proved an illusion easily dispelled, leaving behind the reality of our total vulnerability. Within a week of the war's outbreak, refugees started arriving at INERA from smaller camps in the region. Many were badly hurt, and their stories drove fear into all of us. Our Rwandan broth-ers, together with their rebel allies, had attacked the camps with machine guns and rockets. There had been Hutu fighters hiding among the refugees, but it was not just the militias being targeted. The invading soldiers were trying to kill everyone.

It was when our school was closed down, along with all others in the area, that I started to feel really afraid. The new arrivals said death wasn't the worst thing that could happen to you. The rebels would shoot you in the leg so you'd be left behind, and then they'd torture you. I would lie awake at night imagin-ing this. If I did fall asleep, I dreamed I had lost the

capacity to move. Powerful downpours punctu-
ated hot and humid days. Some among us spoke of
fleeing, but none knew in which direction to go. If
other *bakimbizi* were coming here for safety, then
where should we run? Still, we kept our bags ready.

Only Papa seemed calm. If anyone expressed
fear, he would say, "Let us pray and ask God to
be the judge." So we would hold hands and close
our eyes.

Many believed the blood of Tutsis killed was
crying out to God, and He was avenging on their
behalf. My dad, being who he was, believed that
something as horrible as genocide could not go
unnoticed, and unpunished, by God. He would
therefore pray for God to forgive our sins and
the sins of our fellow Rwandans. Back then, I did
not understand: Why, since we had done nothing
wrong, did he ask for forgiveness? But now I do.

DEPARTMENT OF
HOMELAND SECURITY

CHICAGO, IL

* * *

FEBRUARY 2014

A uniformed officer entered the waiting room. She carried a large metal tray of sandwiches and rows of paper cups of water. We had not been given breakfast before we left for Chicago, and I was hungry, a feeling exacerbated by the cold.

I went over and took a sandwich but found I could not eat it. The smell from the toilet in the corner was making me nauseous. I pressed one of the cold, soft paper cups to my lips, but I could not drink, either.

Ever since the forest, certain scents will trigger extreme physical responses. When I smell them, part of me goes back to that march and there is no convincing my body I am anywhere else. I returned to my position at the wall, folded my arms again, and tried to revive the meditation on Heaven I'd begun in the bus.

"Set your mind on things above, not things that are on Earth," Paul said in Colossians. Such thoughts, thankfully, were close to mind. With a group of fellow prisoners, I had been studying the Book of Revelation nightly in the rec room.

Revelation was the only part of the Bible we had not read as a family, my dad considering it too mystical for young minds. He called it "a double-edged sword, a message to love and to fear."

When I'd seen two young men from El Salvador reading *Apocalypsis*, I'd asked if I could join them. They had agreed, and though they had already reached the third chapter, they charitably went back to the beginning and switched to reciting in English.

We were allowed two hours in the rec room every evening, and while others watched TV, we studied. One of us would read a verse out loud and then we'd all discuss it. I had never read so closely or thought so deeply about the meaning of Christ's Second Coming.

The more we read, the more prisoners joined us. What had been two and then three became more every day. Soon we were over fifteen readers—a small church behind bars.

We debated especially the famous question of whether Jesus will come before or after the Great Tribulations. Some believed he would come before and so spare his followers the suffering of the End of Days. Others held that he would come afterwards, and the torments of the Apocalypse would be God's final test of our faith.

I always knew my father believed the Tribulations would come only after the Church had been raptured. But here in prison I had a powerful realization of my own. Both theories, pre and post, are plausible. What matters is that we do the work of repentance each day, to maintain a loving heart, permanently humble before God and others. Then we will be ready at any time.

Thirteen

REVELATION

We were in our tent eating breakfast when thunder sent us to the ground. The explosion had been so close and loud that for a long moment afterwards my ears did not process any other sound. When they worked again, what I heard was a thousand screams. Papa got unsteadily to his feet and cried up to God in prayer as the *crack-crack-crack* of gunfire joined the cries and multiplied them. The rest of us remained fixed to the ground where we had fallen. Then, all of a sudden, Sy bolted past Maman's outstretched arms and ran out of the tent, and Joel scrabbled to his feet and went after him.

We stayed, stunned for a moment, in a deeper confusion as we processed what had just happened.

Then we followed Sy and Joel into a world of smoke and billowing clouds of dust.

Terrified people moved as fast as they could in all directions. I saw neither Joel nor Sy. What I could see was Maman running and holding on to Ebe's hand, and Ebe struggling to keep up with her. My mother looked over her shoulder at me. She shouted for me to follow her. But too many people were running, and I lost sight of both of them.

I sprinted alone, not looking back, past the edges of the camp and into the open fields that lay before the forest I could see in the distance. Bullets flew from every side. Blood dampened the ground. I ran and ran, kilometre after kilometre, alongside others running just like me, before it felt safe to slow down, and then I walked.

I was in the midst of a large number of people — maybe a few hundred — all entering the forest at the same time. The sound of gunshots behind us filled me with fear, and I walked on, my heart punching me.

Deeper and deeper into the shadowed forest we went. All around me were people tramping, pushing branches out of their way. There were so many of us.

A group of elders said we were too many; it left us vulnerable to attack. They broke us into several smaller groups and we diverged. Many in my group were wounded, glistening pieces of lead lodged in their blood-soaked thighs and arms. I could smell something warm—blood.

THE FIRST OF my family I saw was Ebe. It must have been late morning or midday, though the skies were overcast, when I found him sitting near a group of people who had stopped to cook. Calling out his name, I sprinted to embrace him. But when my brother saw me, he showed no sign of joy or relief. He just stared at me, trembling. I pulled him close and hugged him tightly. His young body was rigid with fear. I made him look at me, and I said into his face, "Where are the others, Ebe?" He could not speak. "Come," I said. "Keep close to me."

Our group used the noise of bombs and gunfire behind us to plot the course of our flight. There was no plan except to get as far away as possible from the camp.

Despite my fear, there was in me a powerful desire to stop and wait for the rest of our family to catch up—or even to go back to look for them. Others could surely see my body straining backwards. An elder threatened to beat me if I stopped.

"At least you have your brother with you," he said. "Do you honestly think the camp is a good place to return to? Your family will come along this path. Keep moving, young one."

The path he referred to was just a rough trail made by refugees' feet. I obeyed him and continued, Ebe at my side. Though he still could not talk, he no longer trembled.

Later in the afternoon, the old man was proved right. In a clearing, waiting for the elders in their group to tell them when to move, sat Maman and Auntie Abayo, covered in dirt.

They spotted us as we saw them. Maman cried as she clasped Ebe and me to her shaking body. In her arms my brother began to sob; it was good to hear sound come from him.

Not long after that Papa arrived, coming up the trail from behind us. He had his backpack and another bag and had picked up a long, firm stick along the way. When he saw us all he dropped everything and cried out to praise the Lord, making everyone nearby turn to look. Papa surely did not care, and neither did we. Some strangers even joined him in praise.

In that moment I felt a renewed sense of hope. I became confident that Joel was alive and in time he, too, would find us. I prayed fervently that Sy was with him.

When, an hour or so later, the overcast skies

finally broke, a heavy, drenching rain fell, clattering in the forest. Now we could not be sure in which direction to go, as the din of the storm obscured the distant sound of gunfire.

But we could not slow down. We continued through the downpour, trying by all means not to circle back in error. The ground underfoot was soft. Mud and leaves and exposed roots made it hard to walk. Our clothes and shoes were sodden.

Some in our group simply could not go on—pregnant women, young children by themselves, the sick and wounded and the traumatized. They just sat down and we walked past them.

The rain eased towards evening, and now we heard new volleys of shelling. It was far away, like a low thunder behind us. Ex-FAR militia were fighting back against the rebels. Outnumbered and overpowered, ex-FARS, too, ended up fleeing and taking refuge in the forest.

Darkness fell like a confirmation of our wretchedness. So many were hurt. So many were separated from their loved ones. Our group stopped to make camp. We were too hungry and exhausted to go much further, anyway. Other groups had decided to do the same. If we could not see them, we could hear them, hidden not too far away.

Dry wood was hard to find, but some men

managed to build bonfires to keep everyone warm and to scare off wild animals. Hyenas were the ones we feared most. Some people sat up to guard the fires, while others slept. Every so often I heard people shout to chase away wild dogs that came to hunt among the sleeping bodies. Auntie Abayo and my dad had run with their bags, and so we had blankets to share among ourselves.

Sleep felt impossible. The thought that Sy might be alone in the dark forest was excruciating. Papa could not rest, either. I whispered, "Papa." I was lying right next to him.

"Yes?" he said, turning his head to me.

I wanted to ask him if he thought that Joel and Sy were among those who had died back at the camp, but I could not bring myself to form the words.

"Goodnight, Papa," I said. He wished me the same and turned his head again.

The scene in the tent played again and again before my eyes. By the time I fell asleep, I had convinced myself that it was my fault they were missing.

Fourteen

MAI MAI

Our group began our walk again early the next morning, through a forest damp and cool after the rain. We reached a road and continued alongside it. It was tarred but, like most infrastructure in Zaire, dilapidated after years of neglect.

Physical details from the attack saturated each moment, as if I was experiencing it for the first time. But the attack also seemed somehow to have happened to someone else, or to me in another life. Time, like everything else, had been thrown into disarray.

Several rough plans among our group had coalesced into one clear one: head northwest to Walikale as soon as possible. People believed—or perhaps just hoped—that the rebels would not have arrived in Walikale, and we would be safe there while the Zairean forces defeated them and forced the Rwandan army back across the border.

Walikale was about two hundred kilometres away along a road that snaked through the rain-forests of the Kahuzi-Biega National Park.

It was on that road that Uncle Rem found us. Or we found him; it is hard to say. He was walking with his three-year-old son, Noah, tied to his chest with a piece of fabric. In the attack they had become separated from Lucie.

There is a saying in Rwanda: *Blood smells*, which means that family will always find each other. I rejoiced in seeing them, but I longed even more keenly for those still missing.

Far from the tilled fields around INERA, we were now walking further and further into true jungle territory. At every rise in the road we looked out across vast green forests that stretched in a mist-like haze as far as the eye could see.

Kahuzi-Biega is one of the United Nations' World Heritage Sites, famous around the world for its population of gorillas. Others in my group did not seem too afraid of the gorillas, so I told myself not to worry about them. I supposed that avoiding bullets was more important.

On the morning of the third or fourth day after

the attack, when we were about fifty kilometres from the town of Bukavu, we saw ahead of us on the road a group of men who were short but strongly built, every single one of them completely naked.

I had heard of these people, but never had I dreamed of seeing them. These were the Mai Mai fighters. They carried impressive guns but also spears and bows and arrows.

These forests were their ancient territory, and they had formed militias to defend it from invaders. The Mai Mai believed they had supernatural powers that made them invulnerable to bullets.

When we came closer, we saw there were a hundred or more of them, decorated with raised scars on their faces and tattoos covering their skin. My brother and I couldn't stop staring.

"Stay here," their leaders insisted. "We will protect you."

No one was in any mood to argue. When we asked where to set up camp, they told us: "Anywhere you want. It doesn't matter. We are going to end the war."

Even as we were building a rough camp on the side of the road, people from a nearby village arrived to sell us food: cassava flour, cassava tubes, pineapples, beans, yams, and potatoes.

The Zaireans knew we needed food. It was a boon to have thousands of people flocking from camps with nothing but their clothes and a few items. We refugees would buy our food with currency, or trade for it with clothes, cooking pots, and spoons. Papa had cash in his backpack, and he bought some food from them.

Uncle Rem and Noah did not stay long. Rem hoped Lucie might be with other refugees heading north and wanted to go look for her. He begged Papa for us to go with him. "This place is no good. It's too close to the road," he said. "The *inkotanyi** will find you here. They could arrive any time."

Papa did not share my uncle's view. He thought we would be safer staying with the group, and that it would be easier for Joel and Sy to find us here.

Rem had to respect Papa's decision, and he set off with Noah and a group of several other refugees who had decided to travel with him. I found myself crying as they walked off. I did not even try to hide it. I was crying for Rem and Noah, but also for my brothers. I was crying for everything that had happened, that was happening still.

As more people arrived, our numbers swelled again. We were many thousands, so we reorganized into smaller groups, and each group picked

---

* Directly translated as "indefatigable"; what some refugees called the rebels

a chief. The new leaders, after consulting the Mai Mai, asked everyone to move a few hundred metres away from the road into the forest, to be out of sight of the rebels.

Among the thick-trunked trees, people made huts out of branches and grass. There was no plan now aside from waiting, waiting for instructions from the Mai Mai or for the next attack to come. Of Walikale I heard nothing more. Papa prayed for protection, but he was practical too. He gave each of us some cash in case we got separated again.

So many were sick and wounded, and without medicine or much food they died. People dragged or carried their bodies beyond the furthest huts and left them unburied in the undergrowth.

Fifteen

PINEAPPLES

Auntie Abayo suggested we pool the money Papa had given us to buy fruit and vegetables from the village to sell in the camp. She was always business-minded.

The village was a walk of about forty-five minutes away. There was no option but to use the road. It was treacherous, but so far the local Congolese had been kind to us and the Mai Mai had not indicated that they would hurt us in any way.

We left camp that morning without telling anyone, wanting to surprise the family with fresh fruit when we returned. In the village we were received well, and all our transactions were friendly. The villagers were enjoying this new relationship with refugees: at last they could do business without having to walk kilometres to civilization.

We were on our way back to camp, arms full of pineapples, when the quiet of the forest was disturbed by an ear-splitting *crack* that came from the direction of the camp.

Auntie Abayo and I looked at each other in wary despair. This sound was followed by another just like it and then the now-familiar sustained staccato of machine-gun fire.

Within seconds Mai Mai fighters were tearing past us along the road towards the camp. Auntie and I stood frozen, unsure whether to run from the attack or back to our family: a terrible pair of choices.

"Come on," Auntie cried, pulling me towards the camp.

We had not gone very far when *bakimbizi* started to arrive on the road, running past us towards the village. Auntie and I desperately searched among them for our family. Rapid cracks of machine-gun fire were interspersed with heavier explosions. We stopped moving again, terrified.

One of the Mai Mai, naked as a newborn, noticed us and halted. "Come, I will hide you. You won't have any problem," he said to us. "But on one condition." He smiled in a deranged way at Abayo. "You must marry me."

Abayo could not hide her disgust. She did not say anything but simply dragged me away from him, back towards the camp, even as refugees sprinted past us in the other direction.

"I have to find the family first to discuss the matter of marriage with them," she told him, hoping to buy us some time.

It didn't work. The Mai Mai kept up with us. "Here, take my gun," he said to me. "Shoot at me and see for yourself that a bullet cannot kill me." He thought this would impress my aunt. Not knowing what else to do, I reached out to take his gun. Auntie Abayo grabbed my wrist. "No, leave it alone. Just come."

We hurried on with this fighter on our heels. The sound of gunfire was deafening. Thick black smoke had enveloped the camp. We watched as wounded people made their way out of it. My heart sank; there was no way our family had survived this. So much anger welled up inside me that I was unable to speak. The Mai Mai fighter had disappeared, but a man who had camped near our family recognized us and tried to stop me and Abayo from going any further.

"We need to find our family," Abayo told him in desperation.

"At least you still have your legs and you are with

each other," he told us, insisting that we go no further. I saw that his arm was severely wounded—wet red muscle exposed beneath the skin. He supported the injured arm with the other, like it was a parcel.

"We cannot leave them!" Abayo cried.

"Why do you choose to die when God has already saved you?" the man said, his voice breaking with pain. "There are people who did not take this road. They went another way. Maybe your parents are among them. If they survived you will meet them!"

The ground near us exploded with a shattering blast, and the injured man and everybody else screamed as we dropped our pineapples and ran with them towards the village.

It took us only a few minutes to get back there, but the road had been blocked just outside with branches. The Mai Mai had changed their minds about protecting refugees; instead they had built a barricade and were demanding that we give them whatever we had if we wanted to pass.

Most of the *bakimbizi* had nothing except the clothes on their backs. Some stripped and were allowed to follow the road through the village towards Bunyakiri, a town deeper in the jungle. Those who refused, like us, were ordered to climb a wooded hill to one side of the road.

We sat down with others among the trees on the

hillside. All we could do now was wait and watch to see if the others came. I still could not speak. Something had seized within me.

I gazed down as group after group were stopped and searched. Those without anything to give up put their hands on their heads and joined us on the slope. In an hour our crowd grew to several hundred.

A man in a long black jacket approached the roadblock, and I jumped to my feet. Abayo thought I was hallucinating. "Sit down, Obadiah." But it was Papa, I was sure, and now Abayo saw him too. Close behind him were Maman and Ebe: *they were all together.*

Abayo and I shouted at the top of our lungs to get their attention, but they were too far away to hear. With life streaming back into my limbs, I felt tempted to run to them.

Their group also had nothing to give the Mai Mai and were ordered up the hill. Auntie and I stumbled down to them. Such was my relief that I did not want to let go of their embrace, and Papa even laughed as Maman hugged me tighter still.

PAPA TOLD US their story. He had called people to worship, for it was Sunday, and that was when they discovered that Abayo and I were missing.

"You were not there to lead the singing," he pointed out to me, more sad than angry. "I wondered what had happened to you."

I apologized for causing him worry.

He said he was leading the prayers when the first rocket hit. Everyone scattered. Many ran straight into machine-gun fire. The rebels had attacked in a U formation, he explained, to trap as many as possible.

My parents and brother had all fled separately and were lucky not to run into bullets. One by one they had found each other. "Only by the grace of God," he said, and grew silent, thoughtful.

"How many died?" I asked him.

"I have no idea," Papa said.

I often asked that question. I had started to think of these attacks in terms of how-many-dead. I suppose it was a way to put into order in my head that which could not be understood.

"But how many do you think?"

"Many," he said, and then he was silent again.

Over the next few hours, more and more refugees arrived at the roadblock. While the others rested, I continued to watch. One small group of refugees was putting up some resistance. One man in particular was standing up to the Mai Mai. His courage had given those with him resolve, and soon there was a tense standoff. Refugees were shouting and trying to push the branches out of the way so that they could pass.

The Mai Mai waved their machetes in the air and pointed their guns at the refugees. The women in the group backed off but the men, emboldened, kept shouting at the Mai Mai to let them pass. Some of us up on the hill, sensing that something was about to explode, stood up.

One of the Mai Mai had a strange knife with a long handle and blade. He approached the refugee who was arguing on behalf of the group and stabbed him in the thigh—a warning to the others to back down.

I watched as the man's leg started spurting blood. People scattered, and the man's companions brought him up the hill. Blood poured out of him like water from a broken pipe. Someone tied a piece of fabric around his thigh to staunch the flow.

"Niko baratugenza iri joro," whispered a woman near us. *This is what we're all going to experience tonight.* She was not talking to anyone in particular.

Papa heard her, and, realizing how fearful people had become, asked everyone to bow their heads. When I closed my eyes, I saw the long blade enter the leg, the dark blood. So, while the others prayed, I kept my gaze on what was happening below.

A Toyota Land Cruiser, brilliantly white, arrived at the roadblock. When the driver's door opened, a well-groomed man in military gear stepped out, a pistol on his hip. By the deference the Mai Mai showed him, I could tell he was one of their leaders.

The man saw the blood on the road and knelt down to inspect it. "What is happening here!" he shouted. Those praying around me hushed and listened, all except Papa, who continued to whisper with his eyes still closed.

"Nothing, just an accident... an accident," said one of his subordinates.

"What accident?" the leader asked, eyeing the trail of fresh blood that led into the trees at the bottom of the hill. He stood and gazed up towards us. "Who are they?"

I tried to get Papa's attention, pulling on his coat several times, but he had entered a trance of prayer.

The leader walked to the bottom of the hill and barked out an order in Swahili: "Bakimbizi nyote, tokeni mwende sasa hivi!" *All refugees, continue your journey right now!*

People stumbled down onto the road. The only people not moving, it seemed to me, were my family. We were waiting for Papa to finish praying. Sometimes in those days I wondered if Papa was crazy. It was not a thought I liked, but it came unbidden at certain moments and this was one of those times. We sat and waited until he opened his eyes. Then we hurried to join the others on the road.

As we walked through the town, I saw no locals. I learned they had fled into the forest. The only people left were Mai Mai patrolling and refugees who did not want to abandon their sick or wounded.

We had not gone far past the town when the Mai Mai leader appeared in front of us in his Land Cruiser. He drove slowly ahead of our group for a long time and then suddenly sped ahead, only to circle back a few minutes later. He repeated this procedure many times over. Each time we thought he was gone for good, he came back. Why he did this, what he was thinking, intrigued me then and fascinates me still.

The rest of the night we moved at almost a march as we covered as much ground as we could under the protection of our surprise guardian. At dawn we all lay down on the side of the road. When we awoke, the sun was already high in a cloudless sky, and the Land Cruiser was gone.

Sixteen

SWEET POTATO

Every day was the same. We got up. We walked. We slept. We got up. We walked. We slept. At first, we could cover twenty-five kilometres a day. Then twenty. Then, as we became too tired and hungry, fifteen, then ten. No one knew how long it would take us to reach Bunyakiri, let alone Walikale, our still-hoped-for destination.

More than three weeks had passed since the attack on INERA, since we last saw my brothers. For the first time in my life, a feeling I would now call depression descended on me, making a mockery of everything I'd once valued, especially hope and promise. I did not share these feelings with others. I would not have known what to say. But so long as I was with people walking, I walked.

Another week of weary plodding and then we stopped, exhausted, near a town called Burambika, in the vicinity of Bunyakiri. Another large group of refugees was emerging from a nearby forest. Perhaps Joel and Sy might be among them.

There was an abandoned school building not far from the road. The wounded and sick stayed there. We camped nearby in a tent made of sticks and black plastic bags.

One morning, after we had been there for a few days, Papa noticed a man looking at him. "Pastor?" the man asked. My father nodded and greeted him.

"I saw a boy," the man said. "I think he is one of yours."

"Where?" asked Papa, clearly trying to contain his hope.

"Back along the path. They are coming. If you wait here, you will see him."

I felt new promise in the air and inside me. But promise can also mean trouble. I realized, my newly risen spirits sinking, that he had said "a boy," not "boys." Perhaps he saw Joel without Sy, or Sy without Joel.

Papa decided we would wait. Even when hope is slim, we must seize on it. Days arrived and passed, and with them came more people like us than I had ever imagined, a never-ending line of faces. But still there was no sign of my brothers. Each time I saw a child my heartbeat quickened, and I hoped—hope that was dashed the next second. Many children walked alone.

At around noon on the third or fourth day a large group arrived, many of them wounded. Afraid of the forest, this group had followed the open area on the other side of the road, exposing themselves to the rebels' fire. While we had been attacked only twice, their journey since INERA had been one of attack after attack.

Without saying anything, Maman clambered to her feet and started to run towards two odd-looking, mud-covered figures in the chaos of the parade. Two children, one tall, one small, stood still in the otherwise moving crowd.

Oh God—they were barely recognizable. Both so thin and covered in dried mud that was grey and cracked like a second skin.

Maman led them back to us. The two moved slowly, gingerly, like old people, as if to conserve the little energy that remained in their diminished frames.

I stood back as Maman lifted Sy to her chest. I saw how little effort it was to pick him up. When Joel came towards me, for a moment, God forgive me, I felt afraid of him. This fear passed and we embraced, my eyes filming with tears.

I had longed beyond longing; I had prayed to see them, but not like this.

We cleaned the dry mud from their bodies and clothes. It was like scales on their legs, arms, and even the sides of their heads. We picked it off, since we had no bucket or any other vessel to fetch water. They looked like apparitions risen from the earth.

After we prayed together, we sat outside our tent, and Joel began to share with us what had happened since he had run from the tent.

"Rockets were falling everywhere," he said. "I knew it was dangerous, but I couldn't leave Sy. My mattress was rolled up outside the tent. I grabbed it and ran."

Sy sat in Maman's lap, holding tight to her blouse.

"I was screaming at him to slow down, but he seemed not to hear me. I hadn't known how fast he could run," Joel said. "I ran behind him for a long time—fifteen minutes, maybe thirty, it was impossible to know—but eventually he slowed down and we walked together."

A mist-like rain had started to fall, but none of us moved.

"I made sure we stayed with a big group," Joel

said. "Some of the others went into the forest to hide, but our group thought the forest was too dangerous. Instead we wandered from village to village. In the towns we met refugees from other camps that had been attacked in North Kivu. When I heard their stories," he said, "I realized the rebels wanted every last one of us dead."

"But how did you eat for this whole time?" Maman asked. She spoke in a whisper since Sy had fallen asleep in her lap.

"Some people managed to run with a little bit of food," Joel said. "And they fed Sy. They felt sorry for him because he was so young."

Maman looked down at Sy's face. His eyes were closed in perfect repose.

"Sy would approach someone cooking while I hid nearby," Joel said. "I knew they wouldn't give him anything if they saw an older boy with him. Whatever he received, he would eat half, say he was saving some for later, and then come and give the rest to me.

"But people soon discovered our tricks. They saw he was with me during the day and stopped giving him food."

That was when things started turning bad for them, Joel told us. He had to swap the mattress for food. Not much, he said, but it lasted them a few days. They quickly became accustomed to sleeping in the mud.

The longer they walked, he said, the more tired Sy became, until he could barely walk on his own, and Joel would carry him for long stretches.

"He was lighter every day," Joel said. "I knew it was because he was losing weight, but still I thanked God for it. Otherwise, I don't think we could have made it."

Joel looked at us, each in turn. "I thought you were all dead," he said. "I thought it was just me and Sy."

He took a breath, before he replied, "And one night I thought I'd lost him too.

"Sometimes I'd go to look for things to make our shelter," he said. "Sticks and grass and bits and pieces like that, and it was easier if I went alone. I'd say to him, 'Wait here for me.' And he would. But one night when I came back, he was gone." He looked at the ground, remembering. "I waited for a long time, and when he didn't return, I started to look for him. I went from tent to tent, asking if anyone had seen a little boy.

"Some people helped me look for him, but it got late and they wanted to sleep. I was so afraid. I cursed myself for leaving him."

But deep in the night, Joel said, when everyone

was already asleep, he heard a child crying and went towards the sound. "Praise God," said Papa.

"Sy was sitting on a log, holding a sweet potato. I asked him why he hadn't waited for me. He stopped crying. He said he was sorry, he knew he wasn't supposed to move. But a man had asked him to come eat with his family. And on his way back, he'd gotten lost. So he just sat down with the sweet potato he'd saved for me and cried until I came."

Maman pulled Sy's sleeping body closer to her. No one said a word.

DEPARTMENT OF
HOMELAND SECURITY

CHICAGO, IL

* * *

FEBRUARY 2014

From a speaker high on the wall near the door came a name, covered in static, and someone stood up. A guard entered, jangling handcuffs, and led that person out.

I had seen newer arrivals called to their interviews before some of us who had been here for hours, so I didn't know how long I'd have to wait. I wondered if Cabrera, wherever he was, had been called to his.

Cabrera was waiting to be sent back to the Dominican Republic, but his government had refused to issue him with a passport because, at the time of his arrest on suspicion of drug trafficking, he had been in the U.S. for more than twenty years.

Of all the lessons I'd learned from my cellmate,

the most important was an old one: *Appearances can be deceiving.*

When I first saw Cabrera, in the rec room, he looked like the most dangerous man in the whole place, but really he was one of the nicest people I'd ever met. He didn't speak often, but when he did, he usually said something funny, and his smile was so big that his giant beard seemed to vibrate around it.

We'd been put in the same cell after we both got jobs in the kitchen making breakfast. I'd applied for the position because I heard you could earn something this way, and I needed money to phone my wife.

The kitchen team received khaki uniforms, instead of the pink jumpsuits everybody else went around in. We were eight of us on breakfast—two Mexicans, two inseparable Nigerians, two Caucasians, Cabrera, and I.

The job was demanding, maybe because I was not familiar with work that required physical strength. We'd get woken up at 3 a.m. and then stand for four hours straight, except for twenty minutes when we had our own breakfast. And for all that we'd get three dollars a day.

The work was intense, but it made us close. We had nicknames for each other: Cabrera was Compadre, and they called me Mike Tyson, for reasons best known to them. Standing in that waiting room, I already missed those guys and wondered if I'd ever see them again. Even the kitchen supervisors had been pretty decent, empathetic people. They didn't have to talk to us, but they did, and their kindness gave us hope. I'd learned how easy it is to get accustomed to a form of slavery without noticing.

Seventeen

AT THE RIVERSIDE

Beside the Hombo River we lived under a sheet of black plastic, which we secured to knotted branches hammered into the ground. All seven of us — my parents, Auntie Abayo, my brothers, and I — slept in this makeshift tent less than three square metres large.

At night, if it was not too cloudy, I lay just outside the tent, counting the stars and thinking back on the last few weeks, since we had left Burambika.

We had come, soon after being reunited with Joel and Sy, to Bunyakiri, and found it a ghost town, so we'd carried on. We were surviving on what we could forage, rummaging in bushes and fields for roots, wild mushrooms, anything that looked edible or even close. What we found we ate raw, since we no longer had pots to cook in.

It was now November, and many in our group were growing thin. Bones protruded from faces, elbows, and knees. Some got sick from eating poisonous plants. They got diarrhea and were unable to hold anything down. If they were too sick to walk, they would simply lie down on the side of the path and wait for eternal sleep to take them.

Death walked with us, step by step.

That feeling of hopelessness returned sometimes, and when it did, I would look at Joel or Sy to remind myself that they were back with us, and though conditions were bad, I told myself to focus on this miracle and be grateful.

We had heard the rush of the river before we saw it. Obscured by bamboo trees, it twisted like a serpent through the jungle. Fragments of concrete, which must once have constituted a bridge, broke through the dark-green surface.

We were discussing how we might cross when we noticed activity near the overgrown bank. It was a group of about twenty naked men, famished but heavily armed, guarding a great pile of abandoned ammunition. Another Mai Mai militia.

We heard from them the same song we had heard at Kahuzi-Biega: that we should stop, that they would fight the rebels and end the war.

Exhausted and starving, we gave in and made camp. The group that had been behind us had to stop too, and the group behind them. The blockade became a bottleneck. Refugees from the North Kivu camps also began to arrive. By the end of the third day, the settlement was enormous. From the river it reached back almost five kilometres into the forest. We realized how many we were.

By then we also knew that such a large group meant we were a target. We feared the rebels and the Rwandan Patriotic Army (RPA) forces,* and what they would do to us if they caught us. Stories of massacres with knives and hammers had reached our ears.

By day we prayed and looked for food in the dense forest and in some crudely worked fields we discovered nearby. Those who ordinarily tended the farmland must have fled to avoid the mass of refugees. We collected the sugar cane and papayas they had left behind. To make our finds last, we ate like birds.

Our tent was close to the river and the Mai Mai, and each time a new group of refugees arrived the surge pushed us closer.

---

* The Rwandan Patriotic Army is the military wing of the Rwandan Patriotic Front political organization.

WE HAD BEEN there for about a week when a huge group arrived with a contingent of ragged-looking EX-FAR soldiers among them. None had a complete uniform. Some wore only military trousers, others just a military jacket or cap. A few of these soldiers did not even have shoes. Nevertheless, seeing them instilled new confidence in my teenage bones.

These soldiers, who had fled Mugunga camp, thought they were on their way south to Zambia but now realized how far off course they had come. Right then and there, they abandoned Zambia as a destination, deciding that Congo-Brazzaville to the northwest was a safer option.

The soldiers said they would help us get through the Mai Mai blockade. Through the vast encampment, word spread that the signal to leave would be gunshots fired in the air.

One morning I was close enough to the roadblock to watch as the soldiers approached the Mai Mai and demanded that we be let through.

The Mai Mai refused. They insisted that a plan for repatriation to Rwanda was underway and we need not move any further.

The soldiers refused to accept this. There was a consensus among them, and among ordinary refugees, that the Mai Mai were in league with the rebels and would hand us to them for slaughter.

I heard a soldier say, "If you love your lives, you will let us through."

The Mai Mai were well armed, but few in number and weakened by hunger. "Shoot us, then!" they cried. "Bullets cannot harm us."

The soldiers told the Mai Mai to line up.

Joel and I and many others stood as those twenty naked men formed a line on the muddy bank. The soldiers raised their rifles and took aim. The Mai Mai stood their ground, smiling, playful, as if it were a game.

My brain froze as shots rang out and the Mai Mai fell, one after another, like a row of statues pushed over by the wind.

While the soldiers continued to fire at the bodies on the ground, a torrent of activity grew all around me. Those camped deeper in the forest, imagining the gunfire was time to leave, spilled down through the trees towards the river.

We grabbed our possessions and joined the movement of bodies. The debris of the blasted bridge served as stepping stones, and in less than an hour, a hundred thousand people had crossed the Hombo River.

In an endless line we put as much ground as we could between ourselves and the river. The road from Hombo to Walikale was untarred, and on both sides of it the jungle was thick. We followed this road—half walking, half running, often stumbling—all day. When Sy got tired, Papa and I took turns carrying him. By the afternoon we were all bone-tired, our feet and legs burning, but we did not stop until night fell. Then we collapsed on some soft soil mounds beside the road and slept.

Eighteen

SNAKES AND FIRE

That night I awoke to screams. One word, shouted over and over again. I surged to my feet in a terrible fright. As the fog of sleep cleared, I understood what the word was: Inzoka! *Snakes!* The earth was alive. All around me people were beating it with sticks and blankets and anything else they could find. Quick and as long as brooms, the snakes angrily turned this way and that in between those soft mounds.

In the morning many of us lay too still, and before we left that place, men buried the snake-bitten dead under that same soft soil.

"Uku niko twese tuzashira," some said. *This is how we will all die.*

Once more we broke up into smaller groups

of about fifty people each. Many in our group had chosen to walk with us because of Papa. The worse things got, the more people craved the encouragement of holy words.

I did not tell anyone, but it was at around this time that I myself became even more bereft of hope. The initial joy and relief of Joel and Sy finding us had worn away; now it was as if I didn't have anything to look forward to. And what good was it that they were back if we were all going to die, anyway?

Ours was a broken world. I saw babies feed at the breasts of women too sick and too weak to stand. I saw other women, past all hope, leave their children in a crowd and disappear.

It was only the presence of those who walked with me that pulled me onwards — my body drawn by the magnetism of the group and of individual faces and voices that retained their humour despite the grinding horror of those days.

One day I noticed a tall, peculiar man walking alongside us. He had no family and carried no belongings. His stride was oddly loping, as if one leg was longer than the other.

We asked where he was going, if he, too, hoped to reach Walikale.

"I'm going where you're going," he answered. "Wherever you stop, I will stop."

Everything about this man was worn and thin. The strain of those years appeared in his bloodshot eyes and the twitching of his mouth. Yet his voice was clear and bright. "Unless you stop before I feel tired," he said and smiled. "Then I will keep going until fire comes out of my feet."

People laughed and teasingly called him the Firewalker. But every day after that, I made sure to walk close to this man, and his dogged optimism and strange, uneven stride were a balm to me.

The people in the villages we passed were destitute and increasingly desperate—the crises of war had compounded their isolation. Some tried to take our clothes and belongings. Fights broke out. Good people on both sides would intervene and mediate. But mostly we pitied them, as they pitied us.

Eventually we reached the outskirts of a town called Tebero, about fifty kilometres from Walikale. There was no one about; only an awful and familiar stench greeted us. Those who had rags lifted them to cover their mouths and noses.

Once we entered the town, we saw in the streets the gruesome source of the smell. Corpses, some lying in pools of dry black blood. A handful of living people sat on a broken curb, heads hung low. In our shock we recognized them as fellow refugees. We approached them gingerly, but they did not stir. It was as if they had been stunned by lightning.

Some elders in our group finally persuaded them to talk, and they told us, with laboured speech, how the townspeople had demanded their belongings, and how, when they'd refused, the townspeople had attacked them, killing as many as they could before fleeing the town. They'd known more of us *bakimbizi* were on the way.

Some of our group called for us to leave immediately. They were scared the townspeople would return. Others disagreed, saying we should stay and look for food. Our hunger prevailed. We scoured the forsaken homes and the fields surrounding the town but found only traces — some dry sugar cane, a few shrunken papayas. When the stench grew unbearable, we hurried, almost at a run, from Tebero.

Nineteen

SURPRISE VISITORS

For so many kilometres, people had put their hopes in this one place: *Walikale*. But as soon as we arrived in this jungle town, towards the end of November, we realized our hopes had been misplaced. The ring of surrounding hills made the town look like a hidden sanctuary, but haven it was not. Thousands upon thousands of refugees were already here. There was no order. In abandoned schools and churches and houses, on playgrounds and pavements and in the streets themselves, people settled where they could.

Most had fled from camps attacked further north: Masisi, Mugunga, Kibumba, Katale, and others in North Kivu. These *bakimbizi* were astonished to see us, since they had heard there were no survivors of the attacks on the South Kivu camps.

Our situation felt more hopeless than ever. None of the aid agencies were here, as we had hoped. What little food we found in the surrounding fields was barely enough to keep people alive from one day to the next. And almost every hour another group of refugees arrived, aggravating a situation that was already intolerable.

So many people and no sanitation were a deadly combination. Cholera ran rampant throughout the encampment. The smell of diarrhea floated on the air. I saw people like skeletons, curled in the street in pools of their own excrement. The dead were left on the peripheries.

During the day the new arrivals would cross the camp, asking questions, desperately describing relatives they hoped to find. At night they would walk through the camp shouting their names.

The radios that some still carried were sources of wild hope and frustration. We listened to Voice of America–Kinyarwanda. From those disembodied voices I heard about the "difficult plight of refugees," but nothing about the attacks, and I wondered if anybody knew or cared about what we had suffered.

The war in Zaire was depressing. Zairean president Mobutu Sese Seko's army and their militia comrades were no match for the alliance of local rebels, Rwandan troops, and neighbouring states that were advancing westward all the time.

Of the conversations I heard around me, conversations Papa took part in, I understood that Zaire had become a slaughterhouse for refugees and we would be safer beyond the borders.

There was talk of crossing into the Central African Republic. To get there we would go north, through Kisangani, Zaire's third-largest city and the last stronghold of Zairean troops.

Some said Kisangani would soon fall and we should rather head west to cross into Congo-Brazzaville, though this would mean traversing the Congo River and vast areas of equatorial forest.

Still others said it would be safer and wiser to simply stay put in Walikale — that international aid groups, with food and medicine, would soon arrive.

With so many starving and wounded, it did seem futile to continue walking. But Papa was determined to leave and go north to Kisangani.

WE HAD MADE our home in an abandoned school building. A few nights before our planned departure, we were sitting outside a classroom when we heard shouts of my father's name.

We stood and shouted back. Two men came towards us out of the darkness. And this is how

Amos and Jean, my father's two younger brothers, found us.

My father crossed himself as if they were ghosts. Then he kneeled in prayer. After a series of astonished embraces, my uncles sat down with the rest of the family. They were both clearly exhausted.

I knew Uncle Amos, the older of the two, slightly better. He was tall and slim, with ears that stuck out from his face, and as dark as Grandpa. He had visited us in 1991 when my dad was studying in Austria. At the time he was a soldier and had been posted close to Kampi. I had admired the way he exercised every morning. He looked so much thinner now.

Uncle Jean, the last-born of Papa's siblings, was not much older than me. He had also worked for the army. Jean had large eyes, almost girlish in their beauty, and so was nicknamed Masoyinyana: "Calf Eyes."

Before we slept, Uncle Amos recounted some of their journey. With other ex-FAR soldiers, he had been fighting alongside Mobutu's troops. From Goma the rebels had relentlessly pushed them west.

He spoke of helping groups of refugees pinned by the rebels. In one of these groups he had found Jean. Since then they had been together, fleeing ever deeper into the jungle. Amos was despondent. He said he was tired of fighting a war that could not be won.

Jean nodded. He too had lost weight. His beard had grown wild.

That was one part of the conversation I remember. Another concerned the small handgun Amos carried, which had no bullets.

"Why are you carrying a gun without any bullets in it?" Papa asked him.

"I got it from a Congolese soldier who didn't want it anymore," Uncle Amos answered.

"But it has no bullets," Papa insisted.

"What do you know about guns, Pastor?" Amos said. "Maybe one day I will get bullets and use it to protect you."

Papa dropped the subject and spoke about our plans to leave. "But I can see you have had a struggle," he said. "Maybe we should wait longer so you can rest and regain your strength."

But Uncle Amos insisted that we all leave as soon as possible. "We need to cross the Oso River before the rebels arrive and destroy the bridge."

I told him how we had crossed the Hombo even though the bridge had been destroyed. I was proud to tell him. I said, "We could do this again."

"The Oso is different," he said. "It's much bigger. Much deeper. If they blow up the bridge, we'll be stuck."

Uncle Amos told us about a camp called Tingi

Tingi, a few hundred kilometres to the north. He had heard that the aid agencies were there, providing food and medical supplies. That could be a good way station on the way to Kisangani, he told us.

He said that he would come with us, at least some of the way. "It is better to die walking than sit and wait for your fate," he told us.

My uncles' surprise arrival took my mind off our wretched situation. Before I slept, I thought back to those occasions when Uncle Amos had come to visit us in Kampi. He was a talented cook and had made elaborate dinners for us. He would spend ages in the kitchen, asking us to bring him this spice or that herb. My brothers and I would sit in the kitchen, curious. I remembered how he'd teased us. "Soldiers can cook too," he'd laughed. "Don't you boys dare think your mom always has to cook for you."

Twenty

TINGI TINGI

We left Walikale, travelling on a tar road that led north towards Kisangani. We were thousands of reed-thin bodies in a long line stretched to the horizon.

The open country was a relief after so many months in the jungle, and the solid tar was easier to walk on than muddy jungle paths. The tar became hot over the course of the day, though, and since few of us had shoes, we wrapped banana leaves around our feet as makeshift sandals. When the leaves wore thin, we stopped to change them.

After about a week of walking, we came to an airstrip where thousands of refugees had already set up camp. They said they had heard that planes carrying food and medicine might arrive at any time. We were tired and chose to wait with them to see if these planes would come.

Uncle Amos left us here. A group of soldiers he'd met at Walikale had convinced him to rejoin the war. There was a rumour going around that Mobutu's army was now paying ex-FAR soldiers good sums in a last-ditch effort to slow the rebels' advance.

Uncle Jean preferred to remain with us. He was weary and thin and wanted nothing more to do with fighting. He apologized to Amos, who reassured him that he did not mind, and the brothers gave each other an emotional farewell.

The same day Amos left, Zairean government forces arrived in a convoy of jeeps to tell us to leave this place and make our way to Tingi Tingi camp. The rebel alliance, they said, was rapidly gaining ground in its westward surge. We were not safe here.

We gathered our things and hurried from the still-empty runway.

FROM A DISTANCE, Tingi Tingi sounded like a bee-hive, the voices of countless human beings flattened to a humming drone.

We stopped at the entrance to the camp and tried to get our bearings. The disorder was profound. Set up amid a blasted, apocalyptic landscape, in which every tree had been shorn of its branches for firewood, crude tents and rudimentary structures stretched as far as the eye could see.

The people there were in bad condition, sitting stock-still or walking around listlessly. Women in their twenties looked like grandmothers, young men like grandfathers. Unaccompanied children wandered around, emaciated and glassy-eyed.

Another airstrip, which started at the entrance, where we stood, ran through the middle of the settlement like a spine. From one of the stalls lining the strip, someone was coming towards us. It was a bald man with a large chest, shaking his head incredulously. Uncle Rem. He had lost a lot of weight.

We did not have the energy to celebrate. My uncle simply held on to my mother's hand and pointed back to his stall alongside the strip. He had chosen this spot to sell cooked rice, he said, because from here he could watch all the refugees arriving. He had heard about the massacre at Kahuzi-Biega, where he had left us, but had not lost hope of seeing us again. He came early each day and stayed until dark.

"Come," he said. "Come and see Lucie."

As we walked, he told us how he'd found Lucie in the forest with a group heading north. That she was heavily pregnant had made tracking her down much easier. They had followed the Congo-Nile

Divide together. For a while they, too, had set their sights on Walikale, but given the speed at which the rebels were advancing, they chose to come here instead.

Lucie sat outside a small tent. At her breast a tiny baby was feeding. Rem smiled. Noah stared at us intently. The baby was a little girl. They had called her Zawadi, which means "Gift." That afternoon I went with Papa to find plastic sheeting; we hung it from branches that we cut from a thorny tree to build an extension to their tent for Jean, Abayo, my parents, my brothers, and me. I felt impressed with our construction but also sad at how good we had become at this life, at how little we asked of the world.

THE TENTS OF the aid agencies stood out from the others: large and sturdy, constructed with metal poles and tarpaulins, not branches and plastic. From a large khaki tent, I saw a white flag with the insignia of UNICEF on it. Outside the MSF tent, where medicine was available, long queues stretched all day and night. I saw the banner of the WFP flying above two enormous tents that served as storage warehouses.

Every few days a plane would land with a cargo of burlap sacks heavy with dried maize and peas. We stood alongside the central strip, next to Rem's stall, and watched the planes land, offload, and take off again. I thought about what it would be like to fly one of those planes and not be just another person waiting on the ground for food.

It broke my heart to see people fight over the pitiful rations coming in. Distribution often devolved into chaos and ill feelings, people shouting that the allotments were too small. The aid workers, mostly local Zairean volunteers, were patient, though. They seemed genuinely empathetic. I still remember their sad, compassionate smiles, especially when helping us young ones.

PAPA REMAINED FOCUSED on God and prayed for hours in the morning and evening. The rest of us split the earthly chores. Auntie Abayo and Uncle Jean were tasked with collecting firewood, while Joel and I were in charge of water.

Fetching water from the UNHCR tanks was difficult and sometimes treacherous, because there was never enough to go around. Instead we walked with a plastic bucket to a stream about a kilometre from our tent.

The truth was that the camp needed more food, more water, more medicine, and even if there *had* been more, for many of us who were already so sick and frail, it would have been too late. I could see my brothers' ribs protruding, and their necks were so delicate that their heads looked like balloons. Ebe especially was so thin that seeing him stopped my heart.

The UNHCR was doing a survey. Volunteers counted the inhabitants of each tent, daubing the exteriors with paint as a sign that those inside had been checked. A hundred and seventy thousand of us, the report said,[*] a city of skeletons.

No bullets flying at our heads was a relief, but the lack of a plan to repatriate us to Rwanda wore us all down. Important people from the European Commission and the UNHCR regularly flew into the camp and walked around, but nothing came of these visits.

In my heart, I knew Tingi Tingi would be just a temporary break before we continued to roam the jungles.

Weeks passed. Talk of the rebels arose and fell away, though it never disappeared completely. We would hear they were gaining ground, planning an all-out attack on the government soldiers' base at Kisangani. The front line was close. We were trapped.

---

[*] See Wendy Lubetkin, "Thousands of Refugees On Road from Tingi-Tingi to Kisangani," *Relief Web* (4 March 1997): https://reliefweb.int/report/democratic-republic-congo/thousands-refugees-road-tingi-tingi-kisangani.

When those conversations would die away, I heard people talk about returning to Rwanda. It had been two years since the genocide. Some thought it was time to go home even without a repatriation plan, despite the risks. This refugee life was killing us anyway, they argued. We needed the United Nations to co-ordinate a robust and multidimensional effort to ensure the safety and human rights of refugees were respected. Unfortunately, we did not know we were the wretched of the Earth, in the words of Frantz Fanon.

Others, like my father, felt it was madness for Hutus to return. If our country's new leaders were trying to exterminate us here, why would we go back into their hands? He believed we needed to wait for the international community to ensure our safety.

These debates did not give me much hope, and the thought that I would never see my country again depressed me. I missed my friends. I missed school. I wanted this whole mess to end.

I distracted myself by helping my uncle at his stall. He bought bags of rice from Congolese who came to Tingi Tingi from Lubutu, a town seven kilometres away, and my mom and Lucie cooked it in large pots. What he did not sell, the family ate, but Rem almost always returned with empty pots.

One day, collecting water at the stream, I met a girl from Gikongoro, one of Rwanda's former provinces. She asked me about life in Rwanda, and I told her, happy of the chance to speak of home. She in turn told me of Gikongoro.

We were close to the same age, but she was alone at Tingi Tingi, the only one of her family to survive the fighting. We arranged to meet again.

In the following weeks, she and I often sat by the stream and spoke of our lives before exile. I thought she was very beautiful. She was dark-skinned, with a gap between her front teeth that I liked to see when she smiled.

This was the first time I fell in love. When we were not together, I waited to see her. When I was with her, time passed too quickly.

I think she loved me back, but I was very naive and did not know how to show my feelings. We held hands a couple of times and she would lean her head on my shoulder for five, sometimes ten, minutes, saying nothing.

Twenty-One

THE BRIDGE

Messengers moved quickly and quietly between tents: a band of rebel scouts had been apprehended near the camp, and they had confessed that an attack was imminent. We must be ready to leave at a moment's notice.

By now we had sold or lost most of our possessions, so there was not much packing to do, only one bag with a few clothes and blankets, and a cooking pot. We still had an allotment of maize and peas, and Papa gave a sack each to Joel, Jean, and me.

The next day we waited, restlessly, for more news. At around 6 p.m., the light failing, word spread through the camp — *time to go* — and as if carried by a wave, thousands began to move along the airstrip. Young and old lugged sacks of maize and what few belongings they had left—pots, jerry cans, blankets, foam mattresses tied to backs.

"Stay close together, boys," Papa said to me and my brothers. "That's your job. And keep moving."

Only a few thousand remained behind—too sick or too tired to move.[*]

Kisangani was about 250 kilometres away. That would be our first destination. From there, if we were lucky, we would continue north and cross the border into the Central African Republic.

We walked into the night, an endless caravan of people. I battled the dark under the sack of maize. We were all weak. Sometimes we would need to stop and rest for ten or fifteen minutes before setting off again.

It seemed to happen from one moment to the next: I looked around, scanning the moonlit faces, and I could not see the others. In all the stopping and starting, I had become separated from my family.

They could not have gone far, but now I faced a dilemma: Should I wait for them in one spot or

---

[*] See "Report of the Mapping Exercise documenting the most serious violations of human rights and international humanitarian law committed within the territory of the Democratic Republic of the Congo between March 1993 and June 2003," United Nations Human Rights Office of the High Commissioner (August 2010), p. 331: https://www.ohchr.org/Documents/Countries/CD/DRC_MAPPING_REPORT_FINAL_EN.pdf.

continue walking? I chose to carry on, but by the time the sun rose, I had not found them. It was slow-going in the dark, and we had only managed to cover about seven kilometres.

The town of Lubutu lay ahead of us in the dawn. We could see it on the other side of a fast-flowing river, swollen with rain. Once we crossed, I decided, I would wait for my family in the town.

Uniformed soldiers guarded the bridge, a long stretch of metal and wood. Their uniforms identified them as Mobutu's troops. It was a relief to see them. They were letting only a few people cross at a time. If too many went at once, they said, the bridge might collapse.

Hours passed, the day brightened, the number of people waiting grew. Some ex-FAR soldiers, who had become suspicious, pushed their way through to speak to the troops on the bridge. The Zairean soldiers repeated their concern that the bridge was not strong and it would collapse if too many people crossed at one time. I heard the ex-FAR soldiers mutter that this was the same bridge that many heavy vehicles had used to bring supplies to Tingi Tingi.

Above us the air was saturated with the whirl and chop of a helicopter. It circled over us, then headed back to Lubutu.

As the afternoon cooled and the light began to

dim, still only a fraction of us had been allowed to cross. An awful idea took hold among us: that these were not Zairean government troops but rather Rwandan soldiers in disguise — that we had been led into a trap.

Panic spread swiftly. Those sitting got to their feet; those standing began to move. I watched in horror as a group of refugees started down the river-bank. Others followed. I was petrified but soon had no choice. The crowd was moving down towards the water, and I along with them.

I was still on the bank when I heard the crack of gunfire and the screams that followed. It came from the bridge. The soldiers were shooting at us.

I crashed into the river. The current was strong, and some people were going under. No longer in control of my movements, I was in a crush of living bodies pushing our way through dead ones in the water. I saw screaming faces and realized I was screaming too.

Someone was trying to calm me. A bearded man beside me in the water said, "Keep going, keep going." I did what he said. I did not stop and I did not die. The crossing took ten minutes, but it felt like an eternity. Then I was on the other side and scrambling up the steep bank, slipping in the mud, over bodies, the dead and wounded indistinguishable.

Cresting the bank, I ran with some others towards the town, using the ditches on the side of the road for cover from the gunfire coming from many sides. The soldiers shot and shot. They wanted us all dead. We hid behind houses, fences, trees — anything that could protect us from this rain of fire.

The shooting had mostly stopped by the time we reached the other side of the town, but we could still hear screams from the river. A group of us continued at a rapid walk. Some exchanged accounts about what had just happened. One of them, a round-faced young man, just a bit older than I was, said, "Even a banana tree shot at me!" and we laughed.

Sometimes I have wondered how that man found it in himself to joke at that moment and how we found it in ourselves to laugh. But that is how it always was. Humour helped us to connect and to share the burden of our suffering.

FOR THE PREVIOUS day and a half I had so often imagined seeing a familiar face that when I spotted Uncle Jean standing on the side of the road, his arms oddly akimbo, I had to look a few times before I was convinced that it was really him.

We were four or five kilometres past Lubutu. I left my group and ran to greet him. Jean seemed neither glad nor particularly surprised to see me. He simply regarded me with a blank expression.

I asked him if he had seen the others.

He did not answer. He just smiled and, peculiarly, sat down beside his sack of maize. I realized that I had abandoned mine on the riverbank.

We had not yet put enough distance between ourselves and the town. When the rebels had killed everyone there, they would surely come for us. I told him we needed to continue.

He refused to budge. I said, "Please, just walk ten kilometres with me. Then I promise I will let you rest."

Grudgingly he stood up. With one hand, I picked up the bag of maize, in which he seemed to have lost interest, and with the other I led him slowly by the arm.

Less than an hour later, he stopped and, without saying a word, sat down again.

I thought maybe he was too hungry. "What if I cook some food?" I suggested. "We can eat and then carry on. How does that sound?"

I borrowed a cooking pot and made some porridge with the maize.

After we ate, we walked for another hour before he sat down again, refusing to go on. I felt so angry with him I started to cry.

"You go on!" he said. "I'll catch up with you. I need to catch my breath." It was a strange relief to hear his voice, even if it was diminished and broken.

Of course I refused. "We need at least another hour's more walking," I told him. "Then we can sleep." We started off again, but just minutes later he stopped and said bitterly, "I want to sleep. Don't talk to me anymore."

I stood and watched him helplessly as he wandered away from the path. He found a spot under the branches of a large tree, lay down, and covered himself with his tattered jacket. Within moments, he was asleep. I went and sat down beside him.

Half an hour later, I woke him. "You've slept many hours. Come on, we need to go."

My ruse worked; Jean put his jacket on and we walked.

But an hour later, he stopped again, saying he was too tired to go any further.

I was at the end of my rope. I was too young to understand how trauma can affect someone—how a person's feet are connected to their heart. But I did not want to fight anymore. I agreed to stop for the night, and we made our bed beneath a tree close to the road. My uncle again fell quickly into a deep sleep; I did not. In fact I lay awake for what seemed like hours, staring up into the branches. In my mind I spoke to God: *Where are you, my Father?* As the sun rose the next morning, I regretted—for the first time ever—seeing another day begin. I wished death had not refused me at the river.

When Jean awoke, we continued along the road.

Twenty-Two

HELLOS AND GOODBYES

The next morning, my uncle had slipped into a still stranger mood. He did not even look at me when I spoke to him. Desperately, I asked everyone we met if they had seen any of our family. No one had.

After about an hour of walking, Uncle Jean was dizzy and unco-ordinated and had to lean on me. Though he was little more than skin and bones, I struggled to walk while holding him on the one side and the sack of maize on the other.

In the afternoon I noticed a bearded man sitting on the side of the road. Although very thin, he nevertheless looked stronger than the rest of us.

When he saw me his eyes flooded with recognition, and I heard him say, "Are you with your family?" His beard covered his mouth completely, producing a comical effect when he spoke. A voice came out, but no lips moved.

"No," I said. "I have no idea where they are. Or if they are even alive." I desired only to continue walking. I was giving up hope that my family was still alive and had no interest in talking to him or to anybody.

"There is a woman who looks just like you," he said. "She was with a beautiful girl. They passed not long ago."

Some solidity in his manner, in his eyes, made me believe him.

I said, "As you can see, my uncle is in bad condition. I can't leave him. Please, sir. Could you possibly go ahead? Talk to them for me. Tell them we are coming."

This kind man rose to catch up to the woman he thought could be my mother. We carried on slowly. A light rain had started to fall. Jean could barely walk now.

About twenty minutes later, I saw them waiting on the side of the road in the drizzling rain: Maman and Auntie Abayo.

I do not know where the man who found them went to, but to this day I think of him with a grateful heart. Sometimes I tell myself he was an angel, or maybe just a man who acted like one.

My mother was overcome. She embraced me. "*It*

really is you," she whispered. I hugged her and then Abayo. Through all this Uncle Jean smiled weakly.

Another refugee, witnessing our reunion, said to my mother, "I know you; you are the pastor's wife. More of your family are close behind. Just wait here and you'll see them."

So we waited in the rain, now coming down harder. Refugees were taking shelter in an abandoned school building not too far from the road.

Soon my father and my brothers appeared. And just behind them came Uncle Rem, holding Noah, and the tall Lucie, carrying Zawadi. We all cried and held one another closely.

Our stories from the bridge spilled out. Maman and Abayo had been among those allowed to cross early in the morning, as were Rem, Lucie, and the children. Papa, with Sy and Ebe, had been on the bridge at the same time as I was in the water. In the crush of people, they were not hit. I told how I had made it across the river and discovered Jean.

By then it was rare to see two people from the same family together. How stunned and grateful we all were to have found one another again.

We decided to spend the night in the nearby school. It was a dilapidated single-roomed structure. The roof leaked badly. A group of refugees were already huddled in the only dry corner.

When they saw how weak Jean was, they gave up their spot for us. Gratefully we accepted and tried to make my uncle comfortable.

That night Jean cried and prayed out loud for hours, asking God for forgiveness. We gathered around him, praying too, offering what comfort we could.

The next morning, Papa told us that Jean was too sick to walk anymore. He said we couldn't carry him, either. "I'll wait with him. You carry on. I'll catch up with you."

"I'm staying with you," Uncle Rem said to Papa.

When Maman and Auntie Abayo also wanted to remain behind, my father became upset. "Please," he insisted. "Please, just move on with the children."

Maman and Abayo knew Papa was right. We had to keep going. I tried to contain my tears, but it was in vain. My heart told me that Jean had a couple of hours before he departed this world. We left them and walked on, at a slower pace than usual so as not to get too far ahead. We walked until day turned to night, and we stopped to sleep. Night turned to day, and we walked again. Like this we went on.

On the third morning, Uncle Rem and Papa joined us in silence. We continued at a slow pace, even though we were not waiting for anyone.

Twenty-Three

CHURCH ON
THE CONGO

For days we slogged north along a tar road that was cracked and crumbling at the edges. Deep, menacing forest loomed on either side. No cars passed, only, occasionally, someone on a motorbike or a bicycle. The Congo River was close by to the west.

Like the landscape, Papa seemed deserted. Burying his younger brother had left him listless. I had never seen him like this. He now prayed many times a day, not just in the morning and evening. He prayed for Jean's departed soul, and he prayed for Ebe.

We were all increasingly worried about my ten-year-old brother. Soon after the incident at the bridge, he had fallen ill, and he was getting worse each day. Papa said he suspected that Ebe had caught malaria. My little brother was always either sweating or shivering. His small body had seemingly forgotten how to control its temperature.

I could see Maman's heart break to watch her son suffer like this and to be so helpless against his pain. She had no medicines to give him, no food to nourish him. We had to try to get to Kisangani as quickly as we could. The city had not fallen to the rebels yet; there could be help for him there.

We were within fifty kilometres of Kisangani— about two days' walk—when we were stopped by Zairean government soldiers. They told us that Kisangani's residents did not want any more refugees to pass through their city.

"You must go to Ubundu," the soldiers ordered. Ubundu was a small village on the banks of the Congo, only a few kilometres from where we were. "Cross the river there, and then continue west. Go all the way to Mbandaka. From there it will be easy to get into Congo-Brazzaville."

And just like that, in one moment, our bold plan to proceed north and eventually cross into the Central African Republic was gone.

What struck me then, and strikes me even harder now, was how readily we followed these soldiers' orders, how quickly we exchanged one destination for another, even though Mbandaka was all the way on the other side of the country, almost a thousand kilometres away.

Our immediate concern was still to get help for Ebe, who was no longer able to walk on his own. Papa and Uncle had to take turns carrying him as we followed the road to Ubundu.

Beyond this haphazard town — made up of crooked streets and ramshackle houses roofed with grass or corrugated iron — flowed the Congo itself. The river was bigger than I had imagined, so wide that the handful of houses on the other bank looked like wooden toys.

The homes had been deserted by their residents, who had fled into the forest after Zairean government soldiers warned that if they mingled with refugees, they would die with us. Since then it had become a refugee settlement.

We found a large church down by the river. Narrow fishing boats were docked next to it. Papa greeted a deaconess, introducing himself as a pastor. "I have a very sick child," he said. "I think he has malaria. Is there any way you can help us?"

The deaconess left to speak to the church's pastor, and shortly afterwards told us the pastor had authorized that space be made for us.

We spent the next few days tucked away in a small corner of the church, beside the pulpit, while Papa did his best to get a hold of medicines for Ebe. Every new group of *bakimbizi* that arrived offered fresh hope — maybe if enough of us gathered, humanitarian agencies would take notice.

My brother's health was worsening. He looked like a skeleton. His shoulders jutted out sharply. The skin on his face was so tight you could see his teeth even when his mouth was closed. His colour was grey. He shook and trembled.

Local leaders arrived one morning and told us to go to a nearby airstrip, where, apparently, planes were scheduled to land with food and other aid. The Belgians had built airstrips all over the country to take its minerals home with them. Many towns in Zaire sprang up around them.

The runway was covered in weeds and stones, and I did not believe that a plane could land on it. But that afternoon one touched down — I recall the word "EUREKA" written on its side — and the pilots offloaded crates of biscuits called "compact food." My dad approached them to ask if they had any medicine. They didn't. He asked if any medical assistance was on the way. The uniformed pilot offered hope there, but gave no details.

Papa did not allow us to eat the biscuits, which

were like protein bars wrapped in thin white plastic. He said he had been warned about them in a dream. Instead we continued to eat maize that he bought from those who had managed to carry it this far.

With new groups arriving every day, we were becoming too many in Ubundu. By now we knew that whenever refugees converged in large numbers, we became a target. We could hear distant bombs and gunfire. The rebel army was closing in from the southeast. We were trapped between the front line and their final target of Kisangani, which was the last stronghold of Mobutu's ravaged army. We needed to find a way to cross the river.

Twenty-Four

THE CROSSING

The ship was astonishingly white. It stood out starkly against the dark-green river landscape. I stared at the thick red crosses painted on its funnel and hull.

We had been told about its imminent arrival but had not believed our informant, a Congolese woman who had come into the church about a week before. Seeing Ebe's condition, she'd told us that a ship from the Red Cross was on its way here. She had heard that it would take sick people to a clinic in Kindu, a town a few hundred kilometres upriver.

The relationship between us and the locals had been improving. They came into the village more and more often to check on their houses or trade us food for money or clothes. They could see the suffering written on our faces.

The woman was right; the Red Cross ship did come, but its arrival brought nothing but disappointment. When the refugees saw the ship on the river that morning, they ran to the bank, shouting and clamouring and waving their arms. As soon as the vessel docked and a narrow gangplank was lowered, the crowd surged forward in a heaving stampede. Only a fraction had clambered aboard when the captain—who must have sensed danger—started up the engine and the ship began to move again with people still hanging on the railings. Some of the refugees managed to scramble on board. Most fell into the shallow waters and waded, defeated, back to shore.

Uncle Rem and my dad then decided that it was time to try something that until that point they had dismissed as too risky. Bamboo lined the riverbank, and refugees had been cutting it down to make rafts. Thousands had already crossed on these rough vessels.

I recall the two of them testing out the raft they lashed together, standing on it in the shallow waters near the bank, while Maman and I watched. It was an overcast morning. Many rafts were already on their way across. When an angry wind picked up, people gathered anxiously beside us on the bank. The swells were rising and the rafts out in the middle of the river appeared to be in trouble. Then someone shouted, pointing, that one had flipped over. I looked and could see people fighting the water.

No one could do anything but watch as raft after raft capsized, tipping the pilgrims into the frightful water. The distant screams and the faces of those on the riverbank will stay with me all my life. On the men in particular, I saw eyes disgusted with life.

There was no more talk of rafts. But we needed another plan. The Red Cross ship had come and gone. The daily sound of artillery was getting louder. The rebels were close.

In the end, the plan came together relatively easily. Papa started going down every morning to where the fishermen congregated to see if one of them would take us across the Congo. The owner of a small boat offered to help us for an ambitious sum. When Papa confessed that we did not have anything near that amount, the man said we could give him our clothes instead. We had no choice. The grown-ups handed over most of the clothes they still possessed. With nothing else to offer, Joel and I gave him our pants, and we arrived on the other side of the Congo in our underwear and long T-shirts.

ON THE OTHER bank we found a few deserted homes and, beyond them, a railway line. It was one of many that criss-crossed that part of Zaire, laid by colonists to bring raw materials to the river. A gravel road ran parallel to these tracks, and we set off along it. This route would take us to the main road going west.

Our group had dispersed, but we were still among many who had crossed the river. As we walked, I gazed at the tracks. It was obvious they had not been used in a long time, years even. They were badly rusted and fallen trees lay across them. But still I fantasized that a train might come. Where that train could have taken us, I don't think I knew.

With no medicine, Ebe had deteriorated even further in the last few days. He slept most of the time, and when he was awake he did not speak. I had learned to recognize death, and that is what I saw in my brother's face.

Day and night we listened to a steady chorus of explosions from the other side of the river. We heard rumours that the rebels were on the outskirts of Kisangani.

And I think this is when my father finally gave up. It was too much to watch his son dying, to know that we were trapped between a rampant enemy and an endless, impossible journey. To get to Mbandaka we would have to travel through the whole country, navigate swaths of cruel forest, even cross the Congo River again. And if we made it there, who was to say we would be allowed into Congo-Brazzaville? And even if we were, what then? *What then?*

"It is too late," he cried late one afternoon.

He stopped in his tracks and addressed the family. Those who were walking with us halted too and listened.

"We are already caught," he said. "There is no reason to continue. We will never make it to Congo-Brazzaville. We have no clothes, no money. We are out of options. If Kisangani falls to the rebels, it is better we go there and surrender."

Uncle Rem, to my surprise, agreed for once with my father's judgement. Joel and I exchanged a look, but we could not argue. Anyway, our own morale was low.

Kisangani was so large that it extended to this side of the Congo. Ferries connected the two sides of the great city. We could make it there in a few days. Surrendering had never been our plan, but nothing else made sense anymore. Perhaps we might even be able to find help there for Ebe.

With a ragged group of one hundred who also favoured this option, we continued on the same road, but with a new destination.

SURELY I HAD known what was coming, but when it happened the very next day, I was unprepared. "It's time to say goodbye to Ebe," Papa said.

He wore a brave face for the rest of us, but I could see his pain. Uncle Rem held Ebe in his arms. Ebe's eyes were closed. His breath barely came out. "Rem and I will stay behind with Ebe until God takes him," Papa said. "You go on. We'll catch up with you."

Maman protested but her voice was small, barely audible. "We can keep going with him," she said. "We all need to be together."

"There is nothing anybody can do now," Papa said. "Look at him. You won't bring him back to life."

"Then I will stay here with him," she said. She began to weep.

"The other children need you," Papa said gently. "They can't go on by themselves."

Maman began to sob so hard she shook. Papa held her for quite a long time.

When it was my turn to say goodbye, I went to where my brother lay in Uncle Rem's lap. I could think of no words to say. I just touched his head.

Carrying our broken hearts with us, we set out. Tears still slid down Maman's cheeks. We walked slowly once more.

Weeks earlier, when we'd left Uncle Jean, I'd known I would never see him again. My brain had understood that when Papa and Rem rejoined us, they would be without my uncle. But when we left my brother behind, some awful fragment of hope remained. If so much had happened that could not have been predicted — so much that was, literally, *unthinkable* — why should Ebe not recover even now? When they met back up with us, why should he not be with them, maybe not healthy and thriving, but alive and walking, like us?

It was just before nightfall when Papa and Rem caught up with us.

DEPARTMENT OF HOMELAND SECURITY

CHICAGO, IL

* * *

FEBRUARY 2014

Outside in the corridor, I heard a woman laugh, and there was something complex in the sound, some sadness at its bedrock, that reminded me of Stacey, my friend in Chicago.

For a moment I allowed myself some optimism and speculated that if I did get parole, it would likely be Stacey who would come get me.

Stacey worked as a public-relations consultant. I'd met her back in 2010 in Rwanda. She was there with her church group. We'd subsequently stayed in touch. In Stacey I had always sensed a deep love for life mixed with an inexpressible pain. This combination touched me.

I had been in jail for a week when I was finally able to let her know where I was, and she'd come immediately with her husband, Gomer. They sat on the other side of a wall in the visitors' area, and I had to talk to their pixelated images on a small TV screen.

But their compassion and care penetrated the bricks. Stacey asked me numerous questions about how I had come to be in jail and my condition inside. She listened to my answers and narrowed her eyes as she processed them. Then she handed over the phone to Gomer. "Your beer is waiting for you at our home, bro," he said.

To see Stacey, even just on that screen, was like worlds colliding. To bear prison, even for a short time, you have to pretend that nothing else exists. Especially the people you love.

A FEW WEEKS after that visit, one of my friends from El Salvador had asked me if I'd made anything for my wife. By the look on my face, he could tell that I was confused. He laughed and said the following day was Valentine's Day.

The truth was, I didn't even know what month we were in. Since my arrest at the airport, I had found it difficult to keep track of time. This scared me. It was way too reminiscent of our time in flight, when I neither knew nor cared what day it was.

The dates on the calendar, just like the people

we love, are anchors that keep us from drifting too far away from ourselves. I thanked my friend for reminding me.

I decided I would make something for my wife, even if I couldn't send it to her in time, and I enlisted the help of another friend who was good at drawing. With a pencil and eraser, he decorated a piece of paper in a way I had never seen before, transforming the page into an antique scroll. On that scroll I wrote a poem to my wife. When I saw her again, I would give it to her in person—a sign of how much I had missed her in here.

Twenty-Five

BENEDICTIONS

The sun had faded my father's long jacket from black to a dusty grey. Time and wear had frayed its edges. In the still air, his whispered words merged seamlessly with the sounds of night. The rest of us were preparing to sleep. He alone continued his benedictions.

For three days, we had followed the train tracks to the junction of the roads to Kisangani and Opara. But no one knew where to go next. On the radio that day we had heard confirmation of news long anticipated: Mobutu's army's last stronghold had fallen. The rebels now controlled Kisangani.

Did we really want to risk going there? We would be out of the forests with the chance to, possibly, meet humanitarian agencies. But the rebels so far had shown only an intent to kill. Why should it be different now? A rough camp formed as people deliberated on what to do.

Papa came out of his prayer trance. He had received instruction. "We need to leave this place right now," he said.

Our companions showed surprise, but those who prayed with Papa trusted his vision. We rolled up our blankets in a hurry and started off again. We had walked about three kilometres when Papa said we could stop and rest for the night.

Papa's vision had not favoured one route over the other. It had just been a message to leave that place. So when, the next morning, we saw signs that we were only forty-nine kilometres from Kisangani, we decided we were so close we may as well go there.

Come what may.

ON THE ROAD that morning we met a group of Congolese wearing strips of white cloth around their heads. They told us that this was the only way the rebels could tell if someone was peaceful or not.

When they saw that we did not have anything white to tear, these good strangers removed their kerchiefs and gave them to us. We tied them around our heads as they had.

A tired but peaceful smile appeared on Maman's

face. "We look good," she said. "Like people going to Heaven." Since Ebe had died, a change had come upon my mother. Now a strange, calm, faraway look lived in her eyes.

It was close to noon — the sun was high in a cloudless sky — when we heard a series of explosions close behind us. We all stopped, looked back, and then continued.

Maybe an hour after that, breathless refugees, some splashed with blood, caught up with us. They told us Opara Junction had been attacked; many were dead.

Uncle Rem turned to Papa. "Your God is real," he said.

What we did not know at the time was that rebel units were moving west and south from Kisangani to find refugees before we reached the city limits. Later they would argue that they feared we were armed.

About six kilometres from the city, one of these units, made up of about fifty men, all heavily armed, stopped us and led us to a military camp nearby called Lula. By then it was late in the afternoon and overcast.

Outside the entrance to the camp, a man in a beret announced that anyone who had been a soldier in the former FAR army must declare so as soon as possible. He spoke in Kinyarwanda — these were our people. I saw my uncle stiffen.

"We have a big task ahead: to capture Kinshasa," the man explained. "We need soldiers. And we know there are many of those among you. Join us and you will receive a good salary. After capturing Kinshasa, you can return home."

But if former FAR soldiers did *not* identify themselves, he said, they would be shown no mercy. He claimed to have documents from the former Rwandan Ministry of Defence that would identify who was who.

With about a hundred other men, Rem stepped forward. The rebels said that the families of these men should present themselves too. Lucie and their children did.

The rebels then escorted the soldiers with their families into the camp. Lucie and Rem both looked over their shoulders as they went in. It all happened too quickly for goodbyes.

Another soldier told the rest of us to prepare to sleep in that spot, just outside the camp's entrance. We were relieved that we did not have to leave Rem, at least not yet.

That night the soldiers told us we would be sent to a transit camp in the morning, from which we would be repatriated to Rwanda.

Red Cross volunteers distributed biscuits, promising that we would receive proper food rations the following day. Once more, Papa forbade us from eating the plastic-wrapped bars. "You will eat tomorrow when we get some real food," he said. "This is not food."

I remembered: he'd had a dream about this too. I was angry with him and his dreams. My stomach felt as if it had been scraped out with a spoon. Papa could sense my frustration, so just before we went to sleep, he threw all our biscuits away.

A drenching rain began to fall. We had no plastic sheets or anything else to cover us. Fortunately the air was warm.

At about four in the morning, I awoke to a stench of human excrement. I tried to go back to sleep but drifted in and out of disconcerting dreams. Dawn's grey light brought with it a scene of devastation. Many of the refugees had had diarrhea in the night and had either died or were on the verge of death. I still don't know why this happened—whether the biscuits were poisoned, as many believed, or just that they were too much for starving people's stomachs to handle.

Oh Papa, your God is real.

THE REBELS ASKED the men among us to help the Red Cross volunteers bury the dead. I was not part of the effort, but my father was. They had no hoes or anything metal with which to dig the ground, so all they did was take a body each about one hundred metres deep into the jungle. Once that horrible work was complete, the man in the beret ordered us to walk back in the direction from which we had come, to another camp called Kisesa II.

Rem and Lucie had come with Noah and baby Zawadi to the camp's entrance to say goodbye to us. My uncle and aunt both hugged me tightly and then did the same for Joel and Sy. Rem whispered a few words to my parents and then he embraced Auntie Abayo. It was never easy for me to say goodbye to Uncle Rem. Maman's brother offered a sense of safety and warmth to those he loved. As we walked away, I thought of us setting off in Akadapfa with Moineau, of how much had happened since then.

Twenty-Six

MY MOTHER'S DREAM

Kisesa II refugee camp was named for the Kasese River, which separated it from its overburdened sister camp. Kisesa II was thirty-six kilometres south of the military base, and the walk took us two full days. Papa comforted us on the way, saying we would no doubt see Uncle Rem and Auntie Lucie again, and until then we could be with them in prayer.

We found another enormous settlement, home to about fifty thousand refugees, so many of whom, I could see, were starving and seriously ill. A horrible sense of slowness permeated everything. People fell every day from malaria and cholera and other nameless diseases. Some would die in their tents and only days afterwards would we smell their decomposing bodies.

Workers from MSF and the WFP, who were based in Kisangani, only felt safe coming to the camp for a few hours a day. The help they could give us was meagre and reserved mainly for the sickest. We heard no further mention of a repatriation plan.

Every morning at 5:30, and again at 6:30 in the evening, people gathered in silence around radios — hundreds around one set — to listen to the BBC World Service or Voice of America–Kinyarwanda.

We desperately wanted news of the war, but even more than that, we wanted to learn that people elsewhere had heard about us. Did they know what was happening? Did they know we were dying? Was anybody going to save us?

Instead, what came out of those small radio sets was soul-destroying. We listened to a minister from the new Rwandan government announce that they had successfully returned every refugee; all those who remained in Zaire were *génocidaires* who needed to be "dealt with." It felt as if the world had washed its hands of us.

Still, day after day the radio batteries would be removed and dried in the sun so we wouldn't miss a report.

I found some cheer in the daily visits of mischievous little monkeys and the chirruping of birds, which to my ears seemed particularly clear in this part of the forest. But such natural gifts could not distract for long from the horror of our situation.

Then two things happened that made this reality even worse.

The first was that Auntie Abayo became ill, her body shot through with aches and sharp pains that became especially unbearable if she moved. It was horrible to see her like this and not be able to help her.

The second was that the aid organizations, whose visits had become less frequent, stopped coming altogether.

All we had to eat now were the wild mushrooms that grew sparsely on fallen trees in the surrounding forests. For safety we would boil them for hours and rinse them three times before eating them.

After three weeks of nothing but a few mushrooms a day, I began to experience a peculiar lightness. I didn't even feel hungry anymore and thought only rarely about food. But at the same time, I could feel that I would not be alive much longer without more to eat.

My eyesight blurred each time I walked to the river to fetch water. I would pause for a moment, close my eyes, and then, after my brain rebooted, start moving again. At other times, a sort of heat would mount in my belly, followed by a feeling of intense nausea, but there was nothing in my stomach to vomit.

The people around me looked like skeletons.

SOME OF THE local Congolese, who were just as poor and hungry as we were, resented our presence, and we often heard angry chants from the road to Kisangani that passed through the middle of the camp.

When three local men were found murdered in the forest, we were automatically blamed. A few days later, some refugees went to beg for food in a nearby village and were cut into pieces with machetes.

We knew that, one way or another, these were our last days as refugees. All around the camp, people prayed to God, asking for forgiveness, for death, for final relief.

I, too, was starting to wish for oblivion. I admit this. But I didn't want to die at the hands of men, like those who had gone looking for food; I wanted to simply evaporate.

"I SAW SEVERAL graves," Maman told us one morning.

She was talking about a dream she'd had the night before. We were sitting together outside the tent. "But five were walking still." She looked at all of our faces. "Five of our family will survive."

None of us spoke and Maman started to cry. "I wish *all* of us could die," she said through her tears. "I want this to be over and all of us to be together in Heaven."

Emotion arose in Papa. Anger, though not at her. "No," he said. "If we all die, who will tell our story? Who will help the people back home understand what happened?"

Maman stared into the ground. She wiped her tears with the back of her hand. Still looking down, she said, "One of the graves was mine."

In Rwandan culture it is a bad omen to be shown your grave. She knew that. We all knew.

"My own grave," she said. "With angels beside it."

NOW I REMEMBER it as occurring later that same morning, although it might have been a few days or even weeks afterwards. I was sitting in a group, listening to the radio, when there came from the forest a giant, echoing clap. The entire camp grew quiet. The radio was turned off. People stood up, held their breath. Another blast, closer, and then another and another, and I watched it as if in slow-motion: people gathered what they could and started to run.

Twenty-Seven

MASSACRE

When I got back to the tent, Papa was calling the family inside to pray for Auntie Abayo, and she was shouting at us with a lucidity I had not seen in days to *go, go, go*. The camp was burning. "I know you love me, but you must leave me! We'll meet in Heaven!"

Papa gave an anguished cry, and then we, too, were running, just as rebels and villagers arrived with machetes and dogs. They hacked at people trying to escape, as the dogs barked madly.

My body found strength from God-alone-knows-where. I sprinted and leapt over bodies and pools of blood. Into the forest, I ran until I could not run anymore, and then I walked, stumbling over exposed roots and the trunks of fallen trees.

We were many in those woods. I asked people around me if they had seen my family. No one had. They in turn asked me about their loved ones. I had no news for them, either. So we limped on, a dazed and breathless mass.

After an hour or so, we were all tired of negotiating that thick forest and we rejoined the road. Exposed and fearful, we walked along it for several hours, until a truck from the direction of Kisangani stopped in front of us. It was carrying soldiers of the AFDL, the coalition that would soon overthrow Mobutu.

We cowered from them even as they tried to calm us. They just wanted to help, they said. "There are people who don't want you to pass, villagers. They have blocked the road up ahead. We are negotiating with their chiefs for you."

Were they being truthful? How could we know? We had no choice but to sit down beside the road and wait.

Over the sound of crying children and distant gunshots, people called out the names of those from whom they had become separated in the attack. I shouted the name by which people knew Papa: *Pastor! Pastor!*

Someone had seen him. *He is back there — Over here.* Information travelled like electricity from mouth to mouth. This is how we found one another: Papa, Maman, Joel, Sy, and me. For long minutes we rested, grateful, in the sight of each other's faces. I could not bear to think of Abayo, left behind in the tent.

As more and more refugees arrived, a fear took hold among us that, far from trying to help, the soldiers were waiting until we were many and then would shoot us all. People got to their feet again, restless. The soldiers angrily ordered everyone to sit down, and those who did not listen were severely beaten. Then, after some hushed dialogue among themselves, they formed a line in front of their seated captives.

The best luck now, I thought, would be to receive a bullet in the head. Papa asked us all to hold hands. Those I grasped—Joel's on one side, Maman's on the other—were trembling.

I watched, both terrified and curious, as a handful of soldiers left the line and began to walk among us, striking randomly with the hard butts of their rifles. We tensed our bodies to receive their blows. Instead, as they came close, we heard them whisper, "Run. Now. Escape."

It took a moment to understand that these were Hutu recruits who did not want to be a part of this unfolding massacre. As we all turned and ran, bullets sprayed into the fleeing crowd like rain. I saw many people fold as they were shot in the back. I heard Joel scream out, "Obadiah! Sha barandashe!" *Brother, I'm shot!*

I swivelled around, but in the stampede of bodies I could not see him. I kept running, unable to stop, following Sy into the trees. Sy was shouting for Papa when he tripped and fell. I hoisted him out of the mud and held him on my side, and like this we stumbled into the forest.

He said he'd seen Papa. "Where?" I asked, and I took us in the direction he pointed, even though I didn't believe he had really seen our dad.

We could still hear close gunshots behind us.

Some time later, it could have been one hour or several, we did discover Papa. He was moving with a small group of people, none of whom I recognized. There was no time to express emotion. I told him Joel was shot, that I had seen him fall. He grimaced and asked us to keep moving.

It was growing darker. A light rain had started to fall. By now the sound of gunshots had mostly died away. The group, no more than sixty people, stopped and made camp for the night. No one spoke. The silence was eerie. Most of these people were alone, or in twos, their loved ones either dead or lost in the forest.

I gathered courage, and I looked at Papa and asked him if Maman had escaped the bullets. He told me God alone knew. But in his face, I did not see any hope.

AS I WALKED alongside my father and brother the next morning, I realized I did not understand God's grace. I did not know why He had spared me, only that He had.

The forest grew even thicker as we moved further from the road. I was aware of no plan other than to hide, to avoid the rebels' bullets, if we could.

It was early afternoon when Papa stopped and said to me that he thought it would be better just to go back to Kisesa and ask the rebels to kill us. He did not look at me as he spoke.

Of course, these words made some sense to me, but to hear them from his lips, in the timbre of his voice, was still so dissonant, so jarring, so irreconcilable with the man I knew, that I was shaken from that waking slumber.

For the first time in our lives, it had fallen to *me* to lift *his* soul—he who had always had more faith than anyone.

I heard myself remind him of what he had said to Maman back at the camp, that some of us had to survive to explain to people back home what had happened to us.

Some others in the group were listening. "If these people decide to go back," I said, motioning to them, "we will go with them. Until then, please let us stick together."

Papa didn't say a word, but we continued on that day, and the day after that. Our feet moved not from will but from some bare instinct. And on the morning of the third day, a man told us he had seen Joel.

Twenty-Eight

JOEL

We were resting beside one of the rough paths the refugees had cut into the vegetation. Another small, ragged group had stopped there as well.

Papa, who was already mourning Joel, thought the man was lying to us.

The stranger must have read my father's thoughts, because he said, "I know you, Pastor. And I know your son. He is wounded, but he is alive. If you wait here you will see him."

Papa looked at me. I said nothing.

"All right. We will wait," my father said to the man. "After all," he turned to me, "we wanted death. If Joel doesn't come, maybe we will be killed."

All I had seen or heard I had told Papa: that Joel had cried out he was shot and then he fell. What I had not said was that I preferred to think of him as dead rather than wounded, left behind to be tortured.

We waited as we had learned to wait: without expectation. A fine mist of rain fell, but we did not seek shelter. No one spoke. Sy slept off and on.

A small group passed us without stopping. No Joel. Then another, smaller group approached, this one only ten or so people, and there among them, just as the man had said, was my brother. His shirt was torn and blood-soaked. A grass sling supported his left arm. The arm itself was wrapped in bloodied bandages made from grass and leaves. His face was expressionless, even as he saw us and drew nearer.

Papa stood, extended one arm, carefully, so as not to hurt him. *"Praise God, praise God, praise God,"* Papa repeated in a whisper. None of us even had the strength to cry.

Using what few dollars he had left, my father bought a cup of peas from one refugee and borrowed a pot and plate from another. I had not seen my dad move with such intention for a long time. I helped by finding a large, flat leaf to divert rainwater into the pot and we succeeded in making a fire under some ferns.

We sat around the glowing wood, warming ourselves, and waited until Joel had the strength to speak. It was an effort for him, but he wanted to.

He said the first bullet that hit his arm knocked him to the ground. That was when he had shouted to me. But he managed to stand up and keep running. Then two more bullets had struck him: one in the same arm, higher up, and another in the side. He went down again.

"I thought I had died," he said now. "I was sure I had. Then I remembered: *dead people can't think.*"

He half walked, half dragged himself into the trees. Blood ran down the left side of his body. A man saw him and begged him to hurry. "Boy, are you serious? Don't you see people dying? Move faster." It was as if the man was blind to the blood and the holes in Joel's flesh. Still, Joel said, at this man's urging, he found the strength to carry on. Remembering this, my brother broke off and did not speak again.

We ate the peas. Joel slept.

MY BROTHER WAS very weak from the blood he had lost, so we walked slowly. The bullet had ripped skin from the side of his stomach, but that wound did not frighten me as much as those in his arm. He held his shoulder at an unnatural angle in an attempt to make the arm hurt less.

Groups shifted and re-formed. We walked with people in the morning who by evening would be gone. When this happened, we hoped they had simply joined another group. Each day we heard gunfire from different parts of the forest. If we thought we were moving towards it, we changed course. The shooting would go on for ten or fifteen minutes and then stop, leaving a silence even more deathly in its wake. If someone nearby still had a radio, we listened with the volume turned right down. When we spoke, it was in whispers.

Some isolated moments from those days of hiding stand out with particular sharpness. This is one of them: It was pouring rain and we had all taken shelter under some thick-trunked trees. We had joined up with some men who recognized Papa and whom we had known since before we'd crossed the Congo. We shared our stories, and they asked us if we had heard what happened at Lula military camp.

Though they did not tell us they were soldiers, they said they had been in the Lula camp but had escaped. The men said that none of the former soldiers who stepped forward had been absorbed into the rebel army. That had just been deception. Along with their wives and children, all those soldiers had been taken into the forest and shot. Papa winced and looked up into the canopy of branches. Rain was still crashing down on the forest.

MY FATHER NO longer spoke of wanting to die, but his heart was broken. Even Joel's return could not change that. A light had gone out in his eyes. Sy was in a world of his own imagination that I could not access. He hardly spoke to me or to anyone, and his face wore a cold, hard expression that seemed far too old for his seven years. Joel's wounds were worsening. A bad smell came from the bandages. A few times I saw him crying silently, although he never complained. I thought constantly of those we had left behind. Of Uncle Rem and Auntie Lucie and my little cousins. I missed Auntie Abayo. I saw my mother's face in the trees and in the shadows of trees.

Twenty-Nine

WATER

Those days of hiding in the forest were not too many, but in our lost and trapped state, with no destination and no aim other than simply not to be killed, they took on a haunted, deathly logic I still revisit in my worst nightmares.

It should have been a profound relief for us to hear, on the radio one morning, that the RPF-backed rebels had at last relented to pressure from the UNHCR and other organizations. Refugees were being told to go to transit camps from where, it was promised, we would be safely repatriated to Rwanda. The one closest to us was back in the vicinity of Kisesa II.

But in the faces of those around me, I saw neither relief nor joy. Many were suspicious that the transit camps were yet another trap. They wanted to hide in the forest until they could be certain. Look at what happened at Lula camp, they said. Some still believed we could reach the Central African Republic.

But Papa was with those who wanted to make their way to Kisesa II as soon as possible. What awaited us there, who could know, but staying in the forest meant certain death. Moreover, Joel's arm was getting worse. The possibility that Red Cross or MSF doctors would be at the transit camp must also have played a part in my dad's thinking.

There were two options for getting there: using the road, which would be quicker but would expose us to rebel patrols, or going through the forest. Some decided to take their chances on the road and left immediately. We were among those who favoured going through the jungle. We rested that night and set out the next morning.

At the front of our group, a few people used machetes to cut the thick vegetation. The rest of us walked in single file behind. We tried to keep sight of the road to give us our general direction. We lost and found it again over and over.

When we came to a river in a valley, one of many offshoots of the Congo that flowed through that area, we faced another dilemma. If we remained this side of the river, its curve would force us very close to the road. Fortunately, we found the river shallow and waded to the other side.

For several days we walked uncertainly even deeper into the jungle, without road or river to give us bearings, until some elders decided we could not continue like this. For all we knew, we were going around in circles. We needed to use the road, despite the risk of exposure. Finding the river again would not be hard.

A NOW-FAMILIAR stench hit us and grew stronger as we approached the edge of the valley. When we crested the rise and looked down, we saw that it was full of corpses.

Papa scooped up Sy in his arms, covering my brother's face with his jacket so he would not be witness to this horror. The ground was cratered where rockets must have hit. These people below had been blown to pieces.

Silently we descended, trying not to step on flesh or bone. It was impossible: my foot slid on a piece of leg—my insides rose and I tried to make my mind go numb. Blank—this was how I must be.

In the abyss of my mind the valley seemed to stretch endlessly. But before long, perhaps after only five minutes, we were on the other side, where the river bent around.

Bodies were piled up all along the bank and in the river too. My stomach heaved as I realized this was the same water we had been drinking downstream. I thought, *I will never be able to drink water again*, and for many years afterwards I survived on juice, Fanta, and porridge.

We waded across and headed back into the forest. I was a zombie now. Each time I returned to that place of detachment, the feeling deepened and felt harder to get out of. We roamed like this for several more days, searching for the road.

Thirty

THE TRACKS

A man on a bicycle was pedalling towards us. We had found the road for only a few hundred metres when he appeared, weaving about. We watched him with a mixture of fear and fascination. He was the only moving thing, aside from us, in sight.

He stopped to warn us of a roadblock up ahead—Rwandan soldiers. He said he knew it was dangerous for us and told us to go back into the forest.

We retreated a few hundred metres into the trees, but no further because we did not want to get lost again. Then we walked parallel to the road for a few hours until we thought we must have passed the roadblock.

We returned to the road, finding it as empty as

before. We sped up to walk as quickly as we were able. The transit camp could not be far now.

The soldier came not from the road, but from the forest. He had a machine gun slung over his shoulder on a wide strap. He was not in an RPA uniform, though he spoke Kinyarwanda. He shouted at us to stop where we were.

Careless with exhaustion and fear, we started to run across the road to try to escape into the forest on the other side, but more soldiers appeared now, moving in from every direction and surrounding our group, guns raised and aimed at us. We put our hands on our heads.

They told us to gather in one spot beside the road. We did. One of them ordered us to throw down anything we had. To this, no one responded.

Enraged, the same soldier shouted, "If you are found with money at the next checkpoint, I swear you will die slow and painful deaths."

A few people, among them my father, dropped the last of their cash on the ground. The soldiers smiled icily.

"Because you are refugees, and you are used to dying," one of them said, "do you think you will die today?"

His comrades laughed while some gathered up the notes and coins.

Instead of letting us pass to use the main road, the soldiers directed us to a narrow path that took us back into the forest. We were told to follow the path until we reached the rail tracks. The transit camp, they said, was along the railway.

None of us moved a muscle. We were too afraid to turn our backs on the soldiers.

"Go now!" one of them screamed, and we turned and ran. I waited for a bullet in my back or a machete in my neck, but all I heard was the soldiers' loud laughter growing softer behind us.

This footpath through the forest was slick with blood and other fluids. Bones lay alongside it. The smell was overpowering; I never grew accustomed to it.

Ten minutes later, around noon, we reached an opening in the trees, and through the clearing, we saw rusted rail tracks. Other refugees were sitting between the rails, cooking something in a pot. They turned their heads and looked at us with empty eyes.

My first thought, even then, was to worry that a train would come.

WE FOUND MORE of an assembly point than a camp. Only a few refugees had built tents — crude-looking, spherical structures of branches and tattered plastic. Most were living out in the open, scattered for about two kilometres on both sides of the tracks. Beside their depleted bundles they sat or lay, staring nowhere. Plastic water tanks had been placed in a row about two hundred metres from one another. At each stood a line of refugees, waiting.

As we crossed the tracks, a group of journalists in bulletproof vests clamoured to interview us. They carried video cameras and microphones, which they pointed towards our faces. Did we look like aliens to them? That is how *they* looked to me, like beings from another world. But that was the moment I finally thought our lives might be spared.

Thirty-One

ANGELS

Our first order of business was to find the MSF tent
we had heard about. Joel was ailing. I could smell a
sharp stench from his arm when he leaned on me.
We found the clinic near the northern edge of the
settlement, a huge white domed tent covered with
MSF logos.

As we arrived at the dome's main entrance,
I saw Papa's frail body go rigid with shock. He
recognized someone — one of the nurses, a young
Catholic nun.

The nun stopped what she was doing and rushed
over to him. She recognized him too, a miracle, I
sometimes think. She had helped treat sick kids at
the orphanage Papa had run at the INERA camp. She
did not embrace him — perhaps because of her holy

vows, perhaps because he looked so fragile — but her face told a story of wondrous surprise.

"Oh, Pastor," she said. She spoke French with a Spanish accent.

She tended to Joel immediately. When she removed the clump of grass and twigs wrapped as bandages around his arm, the smell became even stronger. One of his wounds was moving. The nun suppressed a gasp. Little white worms, maggots, were frantically twisting in the cavity.

The pain showing on Joel's face made me want to cry, but I told myself not to; I had to be strong for my brother. I watched as the nun cleaned out the wounds and put on new, proper bandages. She said the injuries would still need to be looked at by a doctor. She could be in touch with some people to make sure he was taken to a hospital.

Papa said we would be returning to Rwanda as soon as we were offered transport.

"Do you want to go back to Rwanda?" she asked him. Lowering her voice, she told us she had heard frightening stories. Bad things were happening to those who returned. If we wanted her to, she offered to work on a plan to take us to another country.

Papa bowed his head. Her offer had affected him. "Thank you very much," he said. "We know the risks involved. But to tell the truth, we are tired of this life of refugees."

What he did not tell her, but what I knew to be true, was that he, like so many others, was tired of life in general. There seemed no reason to go any further as a refugee.

"We will return to Rwanda. It is our home."

The nun said she understood. She arranged some biscuits for all of us, which Papa finally consented to let us eat, so deep was his trust in this woman of God. Besides, we had eaten nothing but wild mushrooms for weeks; for the past week, we had eaten almost nothing at all.

The nun said she wanted to see Joel again the following afternoon, and she advised us to stay close to the MSF tent.

We slept out in the open beside the white dome with a community of the most seriously wounded returnees. The stress and trauma showed on them, as it did on everyone there. Though you might imagine that we would have felt *some* relief or optimism, most people just sat on the ground staring at nothing. Others walked around mumbling to themselves.

When we stood in line for food rations the next morning, children ran up to me and Papa, clinging to our pants and insisting, "You are my dad! You are my dad!" It was a heartbreaking task to convince them otherwise.

Back outside the dome, we noticed a man looking at my dad, but he quickly walked by. Then he came back, stared at Papa a bit more, and went away again. When we saw him return and stare a third time, my father finally called out, "What is it?"

The man came to greet us. He said, "Are you the pastor?" Papa nodded but I could tell he did not recognize this man.

The stranger said he knew my father had a sister. He had seen her on the main road, making her way slowly, on two sticks, in this direction.

My dad observed this man skeptically. None of us believed him. It was too far-fetched a claim. Abayo was so ill when we left her; Kisesa was under such heavy fire. Papa asked him if it was not perhaps another woman he had seen. But the man insisted, and then he left us.

That afternoon, as the nun had instructed, we went back into the MSF dome. Again she attended to us very quickly. She gently removed the bandages she had wrapped around Joel's arm the day before and wiped his wounds with a cotton swab.

As she worked she told us a truck was coming the following morning to take people to a nearby airfield. She said she would do what she could to see that we were on that plane.

Papa then surprised me greatly when he related to her what this unfamiliar man had told us about Abayo. He had obviously given the man more credit than he'd first let on. Acknowledging at first that it was a faint hope, he said he wanted to wait for her, just in case. The compassionate nurse smiled and said she understood too.

So, early the following morning, we set up our little lookout station—Papa, Joel, Sy, and I watching as refugees came in over the tracks. They arrived in dribs and drabs, sometimes in groups of ten or twenty, sometimes in pairs or even alone. The figures were skeletal, weak, empty of life and its expressions.

She came on the afternoon of the second day. We saw the sticks first, two thin, slightly gnarled branches, mostly stripped of their bark. Abayo, in rags, leaned on them just as the man had described, dragging first one leg and then the other, like almost useless things.

When she saw us her eyes lit up, but so weak were the muscles of her face that she could not curl her lips to smile.

Papa wrapped her near-naked body in his jacket, and we led her, painstakingly, to where we had been sleeping beside the MSF dome. I fetched water for her to drink, and we gave her what was left of the biscuits from that morning.

No one spoke. Abayo herself did not have the physical power to do so. After swallowing a few bites of food with great difficulty, she lay down and closed her eyes. A feeling I could not name was stirring in my heart.

When she awoke, she was able to eat a few mouthfuls more. She looked a hundred years old. She said that after we had left her at Kisesa she had lain in the tent and listened as many people were killed outside. She had heard the vicious barking of dogs.

When the soldiers discovered her, she had begged them to kill her, but they refused. They said they did not want to waste a bullet on someone so sick.

For days and nights she lay there, waiting for death to claim her, praying it would. Outside the tent, there was total stillness. The soldiers had gone.

Whether she was awake or asleep, she said, she did not know, but an angel had visited her. He told her to leave the tent and walk to the road, and she obeyed.

Or at least she tried to. She was able to crawl only a few metres from the tent before she collapsed on her face in the dirt.

Abayo's story was making my heart soar and sink at once. In my head I counted us again, to be sure. Joel, one. Sy, two. Papa, three. And I, myself, was four. Plus Abayo. That made five.

Five in the family were alive.

So bittersweet was this moment. Looking at beautiful Abayo, I knew I would never see my mother again. Five of us had survived, just as she had prophesied. Now the angels would attend to her, the angels she had seen already standing by her graveside in the dream.

"I don't know how long I lay there," Abayo said. "But the angel returned. He came to me where I lay in the dirt, and he told me to stand up and go to the road."

She was only just able to lift her head, but it was then that she saw the two sticks, just beyond her reach. "Whether the angel put them there or not, I don't know," she said. "Even with the help of the sticks, it took me a whole day to reach the road."

I looked at the sticks where they lay, smooth and sturdy on the ground beside her.

DEPARTMENT OF
HOMELAND SECURITY

CHICAGO, IL

* * *

FEBRUARY 2014

The expressions of the other prisoners in the waiting room gave nothing away, like wooden masks that hide the face beneath. Everyone I had met in jail wore this mask until you showed you could listen to them. Then the mask would turn to ash, and the stories would begin.

Some stories had stunned me with how different they were from mine; one because of how similar it was. That was Melchior's story. Since he'd told it to me, I had held it, and the manner of its telling, close.

He had come to find me in the rec room after a kitchen shift, having been told there was another man from Rwanda in the detention centre. He greeted me in Kirundi and I replied in Kinyarwanda. The languages are similar, so we could understand each other. It was strange and comforting to speak my mother tongue here.

Over a few days we took turns sharing the details of our pasts.

Melchior was born in Burundi in 1972, but his family had fled the Ikiza killings* and moved to Rwanda when he was still a toddler. They had lived there until 1994. Melchior held only Rwanda as his home. He knew nothing of Burundi, in fact, except the language of his parents.

In 1994 it was time for them to flee again. Melchior and his family crossed the border and made their way to a refugee camp in Tanzania. Conditions in the camp were bad, he said. Both his mother and his father had become ill and died.

I did not tell him straight away the parallels in my own story. I did not want to interrupt him.

Melchior stayed in Tanzania until, with the help of a program run by the UNHCR, he managed to organize a Green Card and move to Indiana. There he got a job as a truck driver and later married and had two children with a Burundian woman.

He explained that he had been arrested more than three years ago for driving under the influence

---

* A genocide committed by the Tutsi-dominated army against Hutus who lived in the country.

near his home. The U.S. government wanted to deport him to Burundi, because he had been born there, but he refused. How could he leave his children? Besides, he knew no one in Burundi.

I told him my story, over a couple of days. Melchior listened closely, often leaning his head to one side. I saw him cry a few times.

When my story reached its conclusion, he asked if he could give me a hug. The request surprised me and I hesitated. In prison you keep your defences up. You wear your mask.

Melchior suddenly became self-conscious. "In the U.S.," he said, "we hug people to show them how much we empathize."

I laughed at his explanation and felt my defences come down. When we hugged, I could swear that some sort of soothing medicines flowed into my spirit. I thanked him for his compassionate soul.

Soon after, he was transferred to another prison, closer to Indiana, because his sentence had apparently been reduced.

It was difficult to digest his departure. He was a man of sorrow, but we had borne witness to each other's lives, and the feeling he left me with, which remains in me even now, was far from sorrowful.

Another name was called. This one sounded familiar. The Christian name was Mitchell, which was what they called me here. And the mangled syllables that followed could definitely have been an attempt at my surname. The case number confirmed it was my turn.

I stood up. An officer, an older African American man, entered and escorted me out. In the corridor he shackled me again — this time just handcuffs, a relief for my ankle — and led me down a corridor to a room where a young white officer sat behind a desk.

He looked up from his neat stacks of papers and told me to take a seat. He had a narrow face with a pointy black goatee. His tone was friendlier than I had come to expect. "Do you speak English?" he asked, and I nodded.

"Body language is not sufficient," he barked, all friendliness gone.

"Yes, sir. I speak English."

He impatiently marked a box on the form in front of him.

Then, without looking up, he asked me, "Which country are we sending you back to?"

Thirty-Two

FLYING

The nun stood beside the open truck, looking up at us. She wore her usual uniform, a sort of white veil on her head and a blue skirt and shirt. She had helped to arrange all of the details for our return. In the UNHCR tent, which was next to the MSF dome, hung a list of people's dates of arrival at the camp. The first to come were the first to leave. But because Joel was really badly off, she had advocated for us to be pushed up the queue.

The driver climbed into the cab, and one of the UNHCR staff addressed all of us sitting pressed together in the back. He warned us about possible danger on the road, saying that if anything happened along the way, we should just stay in the truck. The UNHCR were worried about Congolese residents throwing stones and sometimes even attacking these trucks taking refugees to the airfield in Kisangani.

The nun waved goodbye, and as her youthful smiling face grew distant, I felt as if an angel had been appearing to us. A beautiful sight to behold, she truly had been our guardian.

The truck rattled along the road to Kisangani. We all sat tight-lipped, cheek by jowl on the back. Sy sat squished between Abayo and my dad. Joel, protecting his arm, leaned into my shoulder.

I was surprised to see Congolese lining the route, singing and dancing, joyously celebrating our departure. Back then I did not understand why they were so happy to see us leave, but today I do. Our presence there had brought extra chaos and pressure to their world. Their villages were full of corpses. Rebel soldiers would mistake them for refugees and kill them in error. They as well were in need of some sort of relief.

We got to Kisangani without incident and our driver drove us down to the riverside. There, next to a long, low warehouse-type building, he rolled the truck onto an old ferry that carried us back across the Congo River.

The Kisangani airport was just outside the city. Several planes were waiting on the wide expanse of grey tarmac, a few bigger jets and some smaller ones. After having our names checked against a list, we boarded one of the large ones.

I noticed the plane's size, but I was not excited in any way—not to be going home, nor to be flying for the very first time. The dream of being a pilot like Chuck Norris belonged to an earlier version of me. I had no ambitions or thoughts of any kind about the future.

I found it surprising that there were no seats for us inside the plane. Except for the small, round windows at regular intervals along the two sides, the flight felt like being inside the back of a large covered truck. We sat on coarse black mats on the metal floor. Auntie Abayo had Sy on her lap. As we left the ground, she pulled him tightly towards her.

Once our flight had stabilized, I got to my feet and looked out one of the windows, down, down, down. Seeing the forest far beneath us like that, just a dense, solid green space, made my mind go blank at first. Too much had happened inside that greenness to picture all of it at once. Then I thought of my mother. That we could leave her behind like this was unimaginable. I had to sit back down. My mind conjured scenarios: possible ones, impossible ones. I imagined that she might have survived and that years later she would return to us. But remembering the downpour of bullets and rockets, I had to admit the the likelihood of her being alive was slight, and my hope would dwindle further as years passed by.

The flight took just over an hour.

It was hard to imagine that everything had happened so close to home.

WHEN WE CLIMBED out of the plane at the airfield in Gisenyi, a warm wind was blowing. I squinted across at Mount Rubavu and at all the little homes with their old iron-sheet roofs that dotted its foot-hills. I looked at the black volcanic soil and the volcanoes to the north. For the past three years, how I had longed to see just one hill of my country.

Maybe a hundred metres from the plane, about six buses were lined up. We were told the buses were here to take us to a transit camp, where we would be officially "processed" back into the coun-try. Beside the buses were a few ambulance vans, and now some Red Cross nurses arrived, wheeling stretchers, to take the seriously injured to a hospital nearby. Joel was one of those; the nun had been true to her word. We told Joel we would see him soon, Papa said a quiet prayer, and then, with everyone still remaining, we limped towards the buses, the wind bringing a film of water to my eyes.

Thirty-Three

INTERROGATION

We were only a few steps from the buses when some soldiers stopped us. Three of them, two carrying machine guns and one holding a radio with a long antenna. They were in a different uniform from the rebels we had feared for years, but they also belonged to the RPA. One of the armed soldiers demanded to know what Papa's name was and why he had fled the country during the genocide.

Papa reached into his backpack, which he had managed to hold on to all this time, and retrieved one of the documents he kept in there: his Rwandan identity card showing his ethnicity.

He did not know that this document, which had played such an important role in the genocide, was now banned. The soldier snatched the card and tore it into small pieces.

"What was your profession before the genocide?" he demanded.

"I was a pastor," Papa answered. "I am still a pastor."

"Why did you leave the country, then?" asked the other one, who had a pistol hanging from his belt.

"The country was in turmoil," Papa said. "Everyone was leaving."

"Not everyone," said the soldier. "Some were just dying."

"That is indeed true," Papa said. He spoke slowly and clearly. He knew we were in a very serious situation.

"You say you are a pastor. What did you do to help?" asked the third soldier.

"I did my job. I served God. I was a chaplain at a school," he said, "and I tried to help some of the children. I did help some of them." He had never looked so tired and dejected. "As pastor, that is what I did."

"*I did my job, I helped many children,*" mocked the soldiers in a cold singsong.

Other refugees looked away, at nothing, as if by noticing us they might become involved.

My father had never spoken to us about the help he had provided at the beginning of the genocide. He must have kept it from us, fearing that we would be in greater danger if we knew.

I felt a familiar fear spread through my body like ice. Was this where we were going to die? Here, in Gisenyi? The closer we were to home, the less likely it seemed that we would ever get there.

Some of the other returnees were being questioned by soldiers, but these conversations did not take long. When everybody else had boarded and we were still standing with the three soldiers, the UNHCR officer in charge come over to see what the delay was. He asked the soldiers why we were not being allowed on. They told him they suspected Papa was "a serious case"—meaning he was one of the dreaded "big people" of the former regime.

The UNHCR officer looked at Papa, appraising him. He said, "Look, I don't know who this man is. But if what you say is true, surely you will have a chance to arrest him at Nkamira?" Nkamira was the transit camp where we were headed.

The soldiers refused and an argument ensued. They wanted the buses to leave without us, but the UNHCR officer said they could not depart until everyone who had arrived on the plane had boarded.

A Red Cross officer came over and weighed in. He

agreed with the UNHCR man's position. Let them go to the transit camp. If he is a serious case, they can confirm it there and arrest him.

But still the soldiers refused to let us go. They accused my father of being a liar. They said that he was not a pastor, that he was a politician. Their eyes were fierce with suspicion.

I felt my mouth go completely dry, as if there were cotton wool inside it. I expected to see these guns raised at any moment. By then, Joel's ambulance had left for the hospital. I remember thinking: *If these men are allowed to kill us, Joel will be alone.*

Another Red Cross worker wandered over, a young Rwandan wearing a white frock with the organization's logo on it. He wanted to see what all the commotion was about. I saw his face change in an instant. "Let this man go," he said to the soldiers. "I know him."

The soldiers turned their still-angry eyes on the young Rwandan. "How do you know him?"

"Pastor was the chaplain at my school, a high school in Kampi."

The soldiers' expressions did not change. They regarded him skeptically.

"Pastor helped us," he said. "Many of us came from mixed families, and he took us back to our families. He thought we might be safer at home."

The soldiers looked at one another, then back at this kid. My dad's former student stood his ground, looking at them expectantly. The soldiers must also have felt the watchful presence of the UNHCR officer and the other, more senior Red Cross worker.

One of the soldiers told us to get on the bus.

Thirty-Four

MY FATHER WEEPS

Nkamira transit camp was about twenty-five kilo-metres outside of Gisenyi. No one said a word the entire trip there. We were all too afraid to speak. I felt like many people were staring at us. The only sound on the bus was Papa's hushed refrain: *Your will be done, O God. Your will be done, O God. Your will be done* . . .

When we neared the camp's main entrance, the bus stopped and two soldiers stepped on board. "Is there a pastor among you?" one asked.

Abayo and I sat frozen in our seats. We stared straight ahead of us. Papa, who had his eyes closed, opened them, stood up, and started making his way to the front.

"He should come with his relatives," the soldier

said, looking at Abayo, Sy, and me. "And the faster the better."

Papa looked back to us and frowned, as if to signal to us not to follow him.

"All of you come," the soldier said, raising his voice.

We stood up, Abayo holding Sy's hand, and followed Papa and the soldiers off the bus, which now continued along the dusty road without us, while we followed the soldiers on foot.

A group of men were standing huddled near the entrance. Several soldiers, some with weapons, one or two other people wearing light-blue UNHCR frocks, and one man in civilian clothing, a tall, fat man, bald and dark and gesturing as he spoke.

As we got closer, the large man turned around to look at us. I recognized him immediately—another pastor, a colleague and good friend of my dad.

The pastor did not greet us, but he came to stand at Papa's side and continued to speak to the group, apparently picking up where he'd left off.

"This man risked his life, and his family's lives, to help his fellow Rwandans," he said. "Without such people, there would have been no survivors at all."

We found out from him later that, after our diffi-culty at the airfield, the Red Cross worker had rushed to a church in town and called him, and he had hurried to the camp to intervene on our behalf. He had become quite influential in the area under the new government, and he knew the soldiers would take his word seriously.

So much inside me was still dead, left behind in the forests, yet at that moment my heart trembled with pride for my father. I also felt relieved; the threat that the soldiers posed seemed to have evaporated for the time being.

The higher-ranking soldiers left us and returned to the camp, leaving only the pair who had been sent to fetch us from the bus.

They stood with the rest of us now and listened as Papa and his friend spoke quietly of what had happened since they had last seen each other. Papa talked about our time as refugees, about leaving his son and wife behind in the forests. The pastor, who was — who is — Tutsi, spoke about losing his own wife and children in the genocide.

What weight we sometimes ask just a few words to bear.

When they had said all they could, they embraced each other and both men started to cry. Their individual sobs merged into one desperate choking sound. It was the first time I'd ever seen Papa's tears. Even after his friend said goodbye and the dazed soldiers escorted us into the camp, my father continued to weep.

WHAT I SAW when I looked around the camp confused me. We had been told that the United Nations was running this process, and I did see UNHCR logos, signs, and frocks around, but I also saw so many soldiers in the uniform of the new Rwandan army, the army that had been trying to kill us on the other side of the border. In whose hands did our fate rest? Starved and exhausted, I could only think about the problem in an abstract way.

The camp was set in an orderly arrangement of large white tents resembling church marquees. Inside, these tents were partitioned into a network of small compartments, almost like rooms. Each had been given an identification number and could fit about five people. Theoretically there was supposed to be one family per room, but because so many had come back alone or in pairs — a mother with a young child, for example — these people roomed together.

The camp authorities, who were a mix of UNHCR staff and Rwandan soldiers, brought us corn and uncooked beans, and we took turns preparing meals over fires in a common cooking area. Each room was also supplied with a plastic jerrycan to fetch water, a bar of soap, and blankets.

And so, for the next two weeks, we lived like this and tried to recover our strength and our sanity. The most important thing, we knew, was to eat as much as we could, even though this was not easy for us. Our bodies were not used to such regular meals.

The two weeks were supposed to give the dual authorities, the United Nations and the Rwandan government, time to process us before we could go back to our towns and villages. That meant filling out forms, which asked us where we were from, where we had lived before the genocide, where we lived during the genocide, and so on. We understood that they were searching for people who had participated in the murders or who had association with those who had.

But stories were circulating that people, men in particular, were disappearing, presumed killed, without having had their guilt confirmed—people who may or may not have had anything to do with the genocide. These are the stories the Spanish nun had alluded to, and as the weeks passed they would become more and more common and more and more feared. A person would be asked to report somewhere and then never return.

What pain our country was in. How broken everything felt. And I could not see a time when it would ever be better. Too much had happened; too many people had died. I just wanted to go home; I wanted Joel back, all fixed up, from the hospital; and I wanted to sleep. More than anything else, I wanted to sleep for a thousand years.

I was so tired. We were all so tired.

Thirty-Five

SCHOOL UNIFORM

The three of us stood rooted to the spot. It was our house, no doubt, but in this skeletal form it looked strange and unfamiliar. Whatever could be removed had been taken: the doors, the window panes, even the roof tiles — everything was gone. Just like us, our home was a shell of what it had been.

The UNHCR truck had dropped us in the town of Gako, the capital of our commune, that morning. Since Auntie Abayo was required by law to go straight to her home in Papa's district, it was just the three of us: Papa, Sy, and me.

From the truck we went immediately into a large hall next to a municipal building to fill out more forms, similar to those we had completed in

Nkamira camp. After this process, which took several hours, we set off on foot for Kampi, our village. It was a long walk; we arrived as the extreme heat of the afternoon was beginning to wane.

Papa did not seem disappointed by the state of his home or the garden, which lay in ruins, entirely overgrown with long grass and weeds with yellow flowers. He took it all in with equanimity. In a short prayer, he thanked God for our return, and then we walked through the door frame, into the kitchen, emptied of everything except dust and cobwebs. Inside, I felt how few we were, how diminished. Six had left this house; three were returning.

Of those who had fled Kampi in those terrible months of 1994, we were among the last to come home. Some of our neighbours had not made it to the border in time to get across and had had to come back. Most of those who *had* crossed over had settled in the refugee camps of North Kivu. Those camps were attacked before ours further south, and they had been forcefully repatriated many months before us.

Without anything in them, the rooms looked smaller and peculiarly geometric, but it was some comfort to at last be surrounded by walls we could call our own.

Over the next few days, our friends and neighbours—many of them members of the church where my dad had worked—began to come to the house to greet and console us. They were very caring and brought things to help us start a life again. One day, some clothes; another, plates and spoons. In the room I used to share with Joel, Sy and I slept on a pair of mattresses donated by one of the many families Papa had baptized. Another family had given us one for Papa and a fourth for our room, waiting for Joel.

It was too dangerous for us to leave our commune to visit my brother in the hospital in Gisenyi—attacks and disappearances by the new government were frequent—but we received regular updates about him. Soon after we'd left Uncle Luc at Grandpa's in Kabalekasha, he and his girlfriend, who was now his wife, had returned to Gisenyi together. Auntie Peace had come back around the same time, too. They agreed to check in on Joel as often as they could. The pastor with the big belly who had helped us outside Nkamira also said he would keep tabs on the situation. Since the hospital did not have enough food, they took turns bringing him some.

Among the many frightening rumours circulating were stories of injured returnees disappearing from hospitals. Our wounds were evidence of the brutal attacks in the forests.[*] Even with that fear, it was comforting to know that Joel was not completely on his own.

I missed him every day. Despite the kindness of our neighbours, I felt alone. Sy seemed to adapt much more quickly than I. He was eight years old now, and with kids his age, he would disappear into thin air every day. They played from morning until night and many of the mothers — Maman's old friends — would invite him to eat with their families. I never heard him speak about Maman, or Ebe, or anything else. He remained a closed book.

Papa was reinstated as pastor at the church, but since there was no money for salaries, he was paid in food — a bag of rice sometimes, or a sack of maize meal — which I usually cooked. Often he and I would find ourselves in the kitchen, facing each other, unspeaking for hours on end. At other times we would talk furiously about every detail of those months in the forest.

In those early weeks back home, it did cross my mind that Maman might still return, that one afternoon we would see her coming up the road and in our

---

* See "Leave None to Tell the Story: Genocide in Rwanda," Human Rights Watch (March 1999): https://www.hrw.org/reports/1999/rwanda/Geno15-8-03.

rapture we would spring to our feet and embrace
her and she would tell us how she had gotten home.

But each time these thoughts arose, I would
have to remind myself of her dream, and I eventually gave up on the idea that I would ever see her
again, at least in this life.

WE HAD BEEN back for a few weeks when Papa
decided that I needed to return to school. His logic
was that if I went back now, I could complete two
trimesters and my average would allow me to join
my cohort in Senior Five.

I knew I had to go back, but I had hoped to delay
until I had put on some weight. I felt thin and ugly.
My eyes had sunken into my skull. When I passed a
mirror or any reflective surface, I averted my eyes.
But I didn't want to sadden him, to add to his pain
in any way, so I agreed despite my misgivings.

A few days before I was due to start, a boy I had
once been friends with arrived at the front door.
I had played with him since we were little; I had
eaten many meals with him and his family, and he
had shared many with mine. We had been in the
same grade at school.

He apologized for not coming sooner. Stumbling
over his words, he said he had known for a while
that we were back. His eyes did not look into mine

but instead wandered over the paint-chipped walls, the roof with its missing tiles.

With both hands he held something wrapped up in black plastic. He held the bundle out to me. "I brought this for you."

I took it from him and unwrapped it then and there. It was a pair of black trousers: the precise kind I needed for school. Papa did not yet have the money to buy me the uniform, and I had resigned myself to attending in the wrong clothes.

Crying was not in my vocabulary at this time, or else I think I would have cried. It was difficult for me to speak. I tried to smile, as a way to say thank you.

"I had an extra pair," he said.

For a few moments he stood awkwardly outside the doorway, which at least now had a door fitted in it. Then he said, "I hope I'll be able to eat your mom's cooking again."

It was not optimism; it was an unasked question. A family he knew with six had returned with three. But it was a question I could not answer. I just looked down at his feet, which didn't move.

Still looking down, I told him Ebe had died. I said I didn't know where my mother was. But Joel was alive in the hospital. We were waiting for his return.

I looked up again. He nodded, his eyes still swimming with questions. Tears of confusion rolled down his cheeks as he told me he would come back to visit.

He left me at the door, which I closed behind him.

SOME OF THE kids at school avoided me. They discreetly changed their paths when they saw me coming. I did not blame them. I would have done the same. I looked like a hundred-year-old man, limping along the hallway.

But not everyone did. My old friend, who had brought me the pants, did his best to welcome me. A French-speaking Tutsi girl in my class, whose brothers, she told me, were still fighting Hutu militias in Zaire, offered to lend me some of her textbooks.

In those moments, in these simple acts of kindness, things began to change. Among my class-mates, in the familiar rhythms of the school day, I could feel the embers of my old self start to burn again. Concern for Joel's safety still preoccupied me and I was finding it difficult to swallow even a mouthful of water, but otherwise, I was seventeen and I was alive.

And then one afternoon I came home from school and saw Joel and Uncle Luc sitting with my dad at the kitchen table. They were talking and at first didn't notice me. In disbelief, I shouted, "Boy, you are here!"

Papa and Luc laughed, and Joel smiled and stood up. He looked so good, so different from the last time I'd seen him. His left arm was wrapped in bandages, but otherwise it seemed normal. He was not holding it at that awkward, painful angle anymore.

I joined them at the table and learned what Papa had kept from me, fearing that things would not turn out as well as they had. At the church office the day before, he'd received a phone call from a nurse in Gisenyi, who had gotten his number from Papa's friend, the pastor. The nurse had not specified why but had urged my father to get Joel out as soon as possible. Papa had called Uncle Luc right away, and Luc, with the help of the nurse, had managed to sneak Joel out of the hospital. They'd spent the night at Luc and Auntie Peace's home in town.

This kitchen, where my mother had cooked, reminded me of her more than any other place. Having Joel back, sitting in it, but not her, made her absence so palpable.

Luc stayed the night at our place, and long after Papa had gone to bed and Sy had fallen asleep curled up at the foot of my mattress, the three of us stayed up late, talking. We did not speak about our year at Grandpa's, about Mugunga camp or dead bodies in the forest or anything from that time. It seemed to belong to another world, better left alone.

Instead Joel told me about the last few weeks in hospital. He told me that the doctors had wanted to amputate his arm, but how, at the last minute, some Red Cross nurses had intervened, saying it could be saved with the proper care.

He asked me about school, how it was to be back. I said it had been tough at first, but that I was getting used to it. He laughed and said he never wanted to go back.

While we spoke, I noticed that with his right hand he held on to his left arm, as though he wanted to make sure it was still there. He changed and redoubled his grip, fidgeted with the clean white bandages. I don't know if he even realized he was doing it.

In the morning Luc would set off for Gisenyi, and that night I slept soundly.

POSTSCRIPT

* * *

The offices of the Foundation for Widows and Orphans were in downtown Mwurire. I had already spent four years in Butare, while I was doing my undergraduate degree, so big-city life, with all its ups and downs, was not new to me.

By this time, my dad was also living in Mwurire, where he worked for the Evangelical Church. He and my stepmom lived in a house next door to my apartment building, and we all saw each other often. They had three kids, the youngest only two years old.

I was passionate about my work and had learned a lot about the needs of orphans in Rwanda, especially in rural areas. My job took me to the forgotten corners of our country, and I saw first-hand the damaging disparities between the urban and rural settings.

In February 2008, by which time I'd been running the program for a year, a group of missionaries arrived from the United States to learn more about the work they were supporting here. I was eager to make their trip worthwhile. We met several times at our offices and also left the city to visit some of our rural beneficiaries.

Towards the end of their stay, I took K., the charismatic leader of their delegation, to a small town a few hours from Mwurire to see a church that was being built nearby. K. was a former U.S. soldier, and right from the start I felt a kinship with this large, good-natured man. Through his grizzled exterior, a soft light shone. In the dining room of our guest house, while we waited for our dinner, K. turned the conversation to me. He said he was curious to know more about who I was. I answered him vaguely at first, but he was good at reading people and asked more pointed, detailed questions. He wanted to know what had drawn me to this kind of work.

There are a few reasons that I eventually answered him as I did: that he was a foreigner, that he was kind, that he was a soldier, that he possessed an unusual mix of hard and soft—it all added up. He made me feel I could let down my guard. And so I told this man what I had learned to tell no one.

I spoke haltingly at first. I kept checking my surroundings, afraid that the guest house workers might be listening. Mistaking my nervousness for shyness, K. encouraged me to continue. What started while we waited for our food went on long after we were finished eating. I was astonished at how vividly memories from those long-ago years came back to me, the concreteness of the details. It was almost midnight when we left the table and went back to our rooms.

In the car the next morning, on the way to see the church, he told me he had stayed up for hours thinking about all I had said. He asked me if I had written any of my experiences down. When I said I hadn't, he urged me to, and then to "get the story out there," as he put it.

I realized how little this good man understood about Rwanda.

THE COUNTRY I had returned to, more than a decade before, was a haunted place. A mood of death and distrust hung over the land like an obscuring and distorting mist. A new war was raging in the north as the government tried to wrest control of the area from Hutu rebels. Thousands more people were dying. Across the rest of country, the army called meetings that were compulsory for Hutus to attend.

They had been going on since 1994, when the RPF took power.

Called Siasa meetings, *siasa* being a Swahili word for ideology, supposedly they were for Rwandans to unlearn the destructive ideas of the past and to become inculcated with the conciliatory vision of the new regime. But people I knew spoke in frightened whispers about these meetings, from which, they said, many never returned. An eerie pun was coined. It was said that rather than ordered to report to meetings — "kwitaba inama" — we were in actuality being called to "kwitaba *Imana*," which means "report to God."

In other words, to die.*

A large part of the ideology of the Siasa program — which was echoed in my school, on the radio, and in national and international political discourse — concerned the recent history of the country: the civil war, the genocide, and the plight of the refugees.

Around the Genocide Against the Tutsis everything resolved and took its meaning. Interpretations were arranged along the lines of a

---

* Killings during this period are documented by Amnesty International; see for example "Rwanda: The Hidden Violence: Disappearances and Killings Continue," 23 June 1998, AI Index AFR 47/23/98.

clear dichotomy — good versus evil — with the RPF unambiguously on the side of the good. The civil war, for example, retroactively became a simple "war of liberation": *The heroic RPF came out of exile to free the people from the evil regime. The ensuing war culminated in a genocide, which they had to stop, and did.*

Of course, this explanation contains much truth. Powerful elements within the regime of President Habyarimana Juvénal, whose death in a plane crash in 1994 had precipitated the mass killings, were genocidal, and the RPF's victory in the civil war did, in effect, bring the genocide to an end. But this neat picture also ignored important complexities. The murderous brutality of the RPF rebels, from early on in the war, was airbrushed out completely. And of course, what came *after* the Tutsi genocide — especially the killings of Hutu refugees in Zaire — was either misrepresented or suppressed. What we had heard on the radio in the forest was being cemented into "historical truth" — that all Hutu people who were innocent of genocidal crimes had returned to Rwanda by October 1996. Which meant that refugees killed *after* that date were Interahamwe and deserved to die.

That this fact had never been borne out by dispassionate observers made no difference. It is estimated, by the United Nations and others, that up to 100,000, and possibly as many as 200,000, innocent Hutu civilian refugees were slaughtered in Zaire. The massacres have been mapped and documented. But anyone who dared speak of this in Rwanda could end up in jail or worse. The official story, with its neat dichotomy, made it easy for the RPF to label all its critics "genocide deniers" or say they had a "genocide ideology."

I BELIEVED, YOUNG as I was, that these distortions and omissions were just a passing phase in the country. It was obvious to me that the ordeal we had suffered in Zaire wasn't a refutation or a denial of the Tutsi genocide; it was just an important addition to the story. Surely the new government, which said it was dedicated to national unity, to healing the wounds of the past, would soon include our experiences in the official history and crimes against us would be acknowledged and investigated.

When this reckoning did not come, year after year, I became disillusioned. With growing frustration, I saw the influential Western powers praising the new leader, Paul Kagame, for his economic successes, without saying a word about his war actions or methods of governing. I watched and waited. Would the arc of history bend towards justice, as Martin Luther King believed? I wanted to believe that too. So I waited and I watched.

Slowly I put on weight, and I observed with joy that Joel and Sy did too. We no longer looked like zombie skeletons. Sy started coming out of his shell. He still refused to talk about Maman but spoke to Joel and me about other things.

We were three brothers now, and we helped my dad by collecting firewood and water and by cooking. I continued to study hard. I had always been a disciplined student, and despite recurring nightmares and a feeling of emotional numbness, I slid easily back into a steady routine of schoolwork. I made academic success my main objective and methodically set about achieving the various goals I set myself. In the final-year exams I did particularly well and received a government scholarship to attend university.

AT UNIVERSITY I had some wise and inspiring lecturers, many of whom were wrestling with genocide trauma themselves. I looked up to them, but such was the fear that the new government instilled in people that even they—teachers who embodied unbiased scholarship and who were committed to genuine reconciliation—feared to say anything that might be interpreted as a criticism of the government or its official narrative.

On countless occasions—whether in discussions in class or outside—I might have broached the subject of my experiences as a refugee, but not once did I do so. Not once did I tell anyone what happened to us in the camps and in the forest. Not once did I dare paint a picture of the last time I saw my mother.

Having worked during my student days as an interpreter for the American missionary organization, I was offered the job, when I graduated, of running their widows and orphans program. I gratefully accepted; it was exactly the kind of work I wanted to do. So many children had been orphaned in the genocide and in the refugee camps, and so many continued to lose parents to AIDS, in part because rape had been used as a weapon in the recent conflicts. Our American funders took a close interest in our work, and I enjoyed being exposed to people like K. and others when they visited. My dad took a close interest in my job too. It was, after all, similar to the work he had been doing all his adult life. In Rwandan culture, it is not common to hear a parent praise their kids too much, but I knew from the way he looked at and spoke to me that he was proud of the direction my life was taking.

I entered the working world with cautious optimism. I knew who ran the show in the country and what was out of bounds, but I believed I could make a positive contribution without sacrificing my integrity. And for a short while this was possible.

The work was rewarding, and with the children I was privileged enough to help and spend time with, I found healing of my own. But it was not long before I got my first taste of how difficult it is to walk this tightrope in Rwanda. The RPF wants allegiance, and those who do not give it are vulnerable.

Eighteen months in, I was accused by a colleague, an RPF party man, of favouring Hutu orphans in our funding. It was an awful time in my life. I felt angry, helpless. Denying the charges didn't help. My accuser's slander only became more strident, and when the tension increased, my father advised me to resign and find a job elsewhere. What he knew, but I did not, was that this kind of reputation assassination is common in the public and NGO sectors, where most jobs are in the hands of a small, government-aligned group. No longer is the country defined by Hutu or Tutsi; it is about who will be most obedient to the RPF.

By standing my ground without being a member of the party or having any government connections, I risked spending twenty-five years in jail for "genocide ideology." Suppressing the part of me that wanted to fight, I applied to do my master's in development studies at a university in Dar es Salaam, in Tanzania, my four-year undergraduate degree allowing me to go straight into the program. Some time away from Rwanda felt like a good idea.

MOVING TO TANZANIA was eye-opening for me. In the sense of relief I felt leaving the country for the first time since we had returned from the forests, I realized clearly what enormous pressure we lived under in Kagame's Rwanda.

I considered putting such thoughts into the emails that I sent to Joel, but I worried that the emails might be read by the wrong people and put our family in danger. Joel at that time was pursuing his B.A. in sociology, while Sy was still in high school.

My own studies were intriguing. I enjoyed comparing the various schools of thought in the field of development, especially when it came to ideas about how to turn poverty-stricken communities into resilient ones. Though I was still fascinated by psychology, my work with rural orphans had made me interested in making a more pragmatic contribution to helping Rwanda's impoverished rural communities. I returned to Rwanda two years later, refreshed and eager to contribute to the development sector of my country.

But the lessons I had started to learn before I left were only reinforced. At several job interviews, where I was clearly the most competent and qualified person, I was passed over in favour of party-aligned candidates.

A friend told me, "Kwinjira mu Bwato." *Get on the*

boat, brother. He meant I should join the party, which would require pledging allegiance to its ideology.

I told him I couldn't. "Although many of their ideas are good," I said, "I disagree with some of what they teach." Even with my friend I didn't dare go into more detail.

I admit that during that time I did consider joining. Life would have become much easier. But each time I considered it I thought of my mother, and I stayed off that boat.

WHILE I WAITED for a position in the development sector, I found a job at a privately run program doing trauma counselling for young people across the country. I enjoyed this work enormously and, despite my frustrations with the political climate, found myself feeling guardedly optimistic. The kids I was working with seemed determined to look beyond the factors that divided them. If they represented our future, then maybe there *was* reason to hope. I made an uneasy peace with the fact that my family's experiences had been written out of history. Although from time to time I still considered K.'s exhortation to "get it out there," I had come to believe that if my silence would help Rwanda in its search for peace, I could keep my story to myself.

In other words, I had internalized the arguments

of Kagame's apologists, in Rwanda and abroad, that allow him to get away with what he did and with what he continues to do. He is the African success story—a man who lifted his country out of the mire to become a beacon of prosperity. So what if crimes are excised from history? So what if the official narrative contains some big lies? For national stability, sacrifices must be made. And if what is sacrificed is the truth, then so be it.

This was 2010, the year Kagame won his second presidential term after opposition candidate Victoire Ingabire was jailed on accusations of genocide denial. Dissidents fled. Journalists were killed. A senior leader of the opposition Democratic Green Party was beheaded in Butare. I lived in confusion, telling myself the repression was all worth it because life under the RPF was indeed good for many Rwandans. But the compromise—disavowing truth for the sake of order—was leading to a deadly sickness in the heart of Rwanda.

OLDER PEOPLE IN Rwanda say, "Ibyiza birizana." *You don't need to fight for a blessing; it comes to you.* Two blessings came to me in quick succession. I got a job with the United Nations, and I met S.

Before the genocide, marriages between Hutu and Tutsi people were relatively common. However, since 1994, it had become a very rare thing for people to even date across that line. Neither S. nor I cared about our so-called tribal differences. What was important was that we loved each other and enjoyed each other's company. We expected our families to feel the same, and for the most part, they did.

Early in our courtship I broke my usual vow of silence and told her about what had happened to us when we were refugees. I wanted my partner in life to know the whole truth. She listened, empathizing with my pain, and in time, she spoke about her own. She was living in Zaire at the time of the genocide with most of her family. But her relations in Rwanda were targeted with the rest of the Tutsi. The Interahamwe killed several of them in Cyangugu.

In these conditions of painful honesty, our love grew, and we set a date to be married.

MEETING S. ALLOWED me to imagine the future in a new way. I could see ahead of me with an open heart. I looked forward to getting married, to being married. "Ababiri baruta umwe," as we say. *Two is better than one.* I believed that it could be so, that from the foundation of our partnership we might find the strength to work and love.

But the contradictions at the heart of our society, the inconvenient truths papered over in the name of stability and cohesion, did not allow that future to come to pass.

One evening after work, two weeks before our wedding day, I was arrested in the street by secret agents of my country and taken to a building behind a hotel downtown. I put on a brave face but I was terrified. I had heard of such kidnappings. Now it was happening to me.

They interrogated me for hours, focusing on the trips abroad that I did for work. They accused me of working with rebels in the DRC, and of being "unpatriotic." When they finally let me go late that night, I was told I had to report to the police station every day for the next month. My hands and legs were shaking. The demeanour of the interrogators, a cocktail of languor and viciousness, and my trembling response, brought back memories of being terrified in the forest, of putting my hands on my head with a gun pointed at my body, of running, desperately, through the trees.

When I told S. about what had happened, she said she would come with me every time I reported to the police station. And she always did.

WE WERE MARRIED in a colourful ceremony on the shores of the lake. The wedding was an island of rejoicing in a sea of trouble. We rented a big tent that accommodated hundreds of people, who ate and drank to their hearts' content. But the festivities came to an end, and the morning afterwards, even as we woke up side by side, the reality of my situation loomed even more ominously.

Several of my friends, who were more experienced than I was with the ways of the system, had told me that if I kept going to the police station, one day I would not return. Disappearances were, and are, eerily common in Rwanda; this is what we live with. I realized I did not feel safe in my own country, and that I had not for a long time.

After hours of difficult conversation with S., I persuaded her that it was best to leave, and I begged her to come with me. So in early April 2012, I packed my bags and got on a plane to Dar es Salaam. And I became a refugee again, this time an unofficial one.

S. made the courageous decision to join me.

Starting life in a new country was hard. The job I found, working for the American organization in a food security program, paid a fraction of what I'd been earning with the United Nations. Our little flat was hot. I had to travel often, leaving S. alone for weeks at a time. My work was dangerous too. Twice I narrowly avoided being hit in the crossfire of terrorist attacks. And so, when we discovered that S. was pregnant only a few months after we arrived, she said she wanted to go home. She wanted to give birth in Rwanda, to be with her mother and sisters.

I understood this desire but explained that if she went, she would have to go without me. She tried to persuade me otherwise. We argued. I told her she was underestimating the determination of the Kagame regime. In the end we agreed that she would go back home and we would make a plan to reunite, somewhere, once the baby was born.

There were nights, suddenly alone in my hot flat, when I excoriated myself for my cowardice. Why was I so afraid of my country? I doubted my choice, telling myself that I was running from my responsibilities as a husband.

But memories of the terror of the interrogation would soon resurface. Those people would kill me without blinking an eye. As a dead man, I would be of no use to my unborn child.

Then the doubts would return, snapping back at me like an elastic pulled to its extremity and then released. What sort of a man was I?

This was my daily bread, a bitter dose, until a third alternative appeared—an idea, I realized, that had been just below the surface of my mind for years, ever since I had spent time with American missionaries in the early 2000s.

The plan now took shape in my mind. I would

apply for asylum in the United States and, once everything was settled there, bring S. and our little one
over.

It was the beginning of Obama's second term,
a time of hopefulness in that country. And I still
believed in the American Dream.

GETTING TO THE U.S. was relatively easy, thanks to
the kindness of my friend J., a nurse from California,
whom I had met in 2006 when she came to Rwanda
with her church group to train counsellors helping
people with PTSD. Getting asylum, however, proved
far more difficult that I had imagined. Even with
the assistance of an organization called Heartland
Alliance, it took me months just to file a case.

I was staying in North Dakota with Smith, a
draftsman and a good friend of K., waiting for yet
another interview, when S.'s younger sister called me
to say that S. had gone into labour. She phoned late
in the evening, and I couldn't sleep the whole night
until the news finally arrived. My daughter was born
in the early hours of February 17, 2013.

I wanted so desperately to be there. I consoled
myself with the thought that I was far from my
daughter only because I was trying to ensure that
she would have a better life than I had had.

Seeing the picture of my daughter on the phone,

I realized I had never hoped for a child. I had never allowed myself to. A deep shiver passed through me as I understood what this meant. In this little girl, I saw myself in the past and in the future.

IN JULY 2013, after six months of interview hearings sending me from pillar to post, I left the U.S. in frustration and returned to Tanzania, where S. and I had agreed to meet. My baby girl would be six months old in August, and I badly wanted to visit her and S. I believed I could go back to Tanzania, see them, earn some money, and then come back to the U.S. to finalize the asylum dossier.

The September 21 al-Shabab attack on the Westgate Mall in neighbouring Kenya stunned the NGO sector, and the job I had lined up fell through, so I was not able to earn anything in that time. But I was very busy. Life in the apartment we rented in Dar es Salaam was defined by a repetitive regime of feeding and cleaning, eating and sleeping, but despite the relentlessness of it, I was never bored. Aside from a sometimes maddening lack of sleep, I enjoyed every moment.

More than anything, having a child changed the way I thought about my own parents. I found new respect for my father, who had tried, in his imperfect but loving way, to give us some of his colossal faith. And I thought of my mother more and more. Many times before then I had wished she were alive to help me make sense of my daily intricate life. Now I needed her to help me understand the art of parenting. I sometimes allow myself to imagine the wonderful role she would have played in my daughter's life.

In December, S. and our daughter went back to Rwanda to spend Christmas with her family, and soon after, in mid-January, I flew back to the U.S. to see what I could do about my asylum case.

AT O'HARE INTERNATIONAL in Chicago, the immigration officer took a long time over my papers and then started interrogating me as to why, on my previous visit, I had overstayed my six-month limit by two weeks.

In retrospect, I can see that I had been careless, even self-defeating, but at the time I could only feel frustration with the system. I asked him why they hadn't told me about my error in Dar es Salaam. Why had they let me fly all the way if they knew I wasn't going to be allowed to re-enter? To that he said nothing. I said that since my visa was valid for ten years, I hadn't thought two weeks would be such a big deal. He said it *was* a big deal and called his superiors.

They wanted to put me on the next plane to

Kigali. I said I had left Rwanda fearing for my life, that was the reason I had come to the U.S. in the first place. If they wanted to send me somewhere, I would have to accept it, but then please, I asked them, please make it Dar es Salaam. Flying me back to Rwanda would be signing my death warrant.

Since I was a Rwandan passport holder, they explained, my request was impossible. I would either have to go back to my home country, or I would be sent to jail in the U.S. and stay there until the government was ready to consider my asylum request. I said I would go to jail. That night I slept in the airport's Immigration Holding Facility, and the following morning, January 17, two cops drove me to McHenry County Jail, one hour away.

THEY DECIDED TO send me back to Rwanda. However, because the U.S. is a law-abiding country, they had to follow due process, including a court hearing before deportation. That is how I was sent to jail as they prepared the court hearing session. A week after my parole interview, towards the end of February, I was called back to the Department of Homeland Security in Chicago to see the officer in charge of my case.

In his office, crowded with papers and yellowing

cardboard files, he unexpectedly told me I was to be released, but with certain conditions.

For example, he said, I had to attend a court hearing before I could work. That hearing was scheduled for October. I also had to give him the address and phone numbers of the person I would be staying with in the U.S. and alert him if I moved.

I had originally planned to stay for two weeks with a friend studying in Naperville, just outside of Chicago, while reviving my asylum case with Heartland Alliance, and then go visit Smith in North Dakota. But my time in prison had upset these plans. My friend in Naperville had had to travel, and Smith, unfortunately, had fallen ill. I needed to find someone else.

I began calling the other Americans I knew, but none of them were able to host me because of distance, personal health, or conflicting schedules. My release had taken them by surprise too.

The person who helped me, in the end, was a pastor I'd met at a church in Naperville. He said I could certainly give them his details and that he would come get me immediately. I spent three nights in his home. The pastor was recently married, and after the three of us prayed together, I shared with them my intentions. Considering that it would be eight months before I could work legally to support my family in the U.S. — and I was not about to take under-the-table jobs — I was going to drop my asylum case and return to Tanzania immediately.

Neither he nor any of my other American friends understood. Now that I'd been released, even if it was conditionally, and seemed more likely to get my asylum eventually, they all thought I should stay and try to bring my family over when the time came.

I told them I needed to go home to my wife and child. It was hard to say much more than that, and I didn't try. The six weeks I had spent in jail had transformed me in ways beyond easy explanation. Something in me had been ignited, uniting spirit, mind, and heart.

Studying Revelation and discussing the mysteries of Heaven in that cold room in the middle of nowhere, I realized I could have my own relationship with God, one that did not need to be mediated by my father or anyone else for that matter. In this way I felt like I had met God for the first time.

And in those barred cells and grim waiting rooms, surrounded by human beings America wanted nothing to do with, my vision of the country that I had held on to for so long had faded like mist in the morning sun. Dignity was not to be found in any country or indeed in anything that could be seen with one's physical eyes. Dignity was inside of you or it was not at all. No one could give it to you and no one could take it away.

These intimations had, in turn, shifted profoundly my attitude to a past that was not so distant. The anger I felt about what had happened to us as refugees, about the people who were taken from me, had been making me soul-sick because the story remained untold. After listening to Melchior's experiences and telling him mine — especially after the embrace we had shared — I understood the healing, both personal and collective, that can come with telling and hearing the truth. I told myself that when I got out, I would actually do it. I would write it all down.

AND I DID. I flew back to Tanzania and spent April, May, and June with S. and my daughter in Dar es Salaam. At night, after they were both asleep, I would sit at my laptop and write. I wrote in French and saved the files on a flash disk that I kept hidden at the back of a drawer. In June, S. took our daughter back to her family in Rwanda. I understood that many things were easier for her there, with her mom and her sisters. Our life was complicated.

I carried on writing. When I got to the end of my story, I went back to the beginning. I started trying to flesh out my notes and checking memories against maps and dates in articles online. I called Rwandan friends who I knew had also been in the refugee camps. Most had left Rwanda, so I felt comfortable emailing or phoning them. I came to the end again.

My story, as I remembered it, was complete. But I was still not sure I would show my writing to anyone. Many times, I considered destroying the disk and forgetting about it once and for all.

Because the massacres I had written about raised the question of a "second genocide" or a "Hutu genocide," I knew how easy it would be to twist my words. Many perpetrators of the Genocide Against the Tutsis—extremist Hutus—try to use the idea of a "second genocide" to legitimize or excuse their crimes. Which, to be clear, should never be permitted. No one must ever deny the horrors of what was done to the Tutsi people in those nightmarish months of 1994.

My own feeling is that too much is made of the question of the "Hutu genocide." Whether or not the killing of Hutu refugees in Zaire qualifies, technically, as a genocide (and readers can make up their own minds, if they want, since enough has been written about it*), surely it is a question that just distracts from the real issue. Genocide or not, enough innocent refugees died at the hands of the RPF and their rebel allies to warrant international recognition, condemnation, and investigation.

But the current government of Rwanda jealously guards its position as the sole holder of suffering. Any person who pushes for recognition of the massacres I have testified to either sits in jail for "genocide ideol-ogy," like Tutsi genocide survivor Deo Mushayidi, or lies dead in the ground, like gospel singer Kizito Mihigo and so many others.

So of course, I felt the chilling effect. How could I not? Even as I prepare this concluding chapter, confident that the book will be published, I am still plagued by fears of what the Rwandan government will do to punish me. But I manage these fears by reminding myself that as long as this conversation is out of bounds, and those who speak about these things are in danger, there is no hope for Rwanda.

WITHOUT A CAR or a motorbike, getting around Dar es Salaam is hectic. I always take small Dala dala, vans

---

* For example, see Scott Straus, "The Limits of a Genocide Lens: Violence Against Rwandans in the 1990s," *Journal of Genocide Research* (2019) 21:4, pp. 504–524, https://doi.org/10.1080/14623528.2019.1623527.

which in European countries serve as ambulances. My life in the city revolves around studying and teaching at a couple of universities. There is also a regular need for interpreters here, so I have been able to find a steady stream of extra work offering this service.

Even though the traffic jams here can be overwhelming and one needs to look out for pickpockets and other petty criminals, I enjoy making my way around the city's streets, parks, and shopping malls. I especially like Java House restaurants. Their food is great and easy on my pocketbook.

I share an apartment here with Sy. My little brother is a musician and a very social person. Sometimes I worry that he and his friends overdo the drinking, but keeping him in check is an interesting journey. His music is amazing, and in the lyrics of the songs he writes, I decipher messages about his lost childhood. He sings what he was never able to speak. Sy encourages me every day, and I can't explain enough how great it feels to have him around.

The life of exile is very strange. I miss home. I miss the food, Rwandan cassava leaves, mashed soft and cooked with beef and eaten with cassava paste or rice. I miss eating a good salad from one of the restaurants in Kigali. I miss hearing my people speak Kinyarwanda in the streets. I miss festivities where people dance to our beats and tunes. I miss the dance called *umushayayo* and the one called *intore*.

THE DIFFICULTIES MY wife and I have faced, the disagreements that stem at least in part from my exile over where and how to be together, are not material to this book. Suffice to say, I would like, more than anything, to be closer to my child, but I cannot go back to Rwanda.

From a distance I watch my daughter grow up in the country of my birth and hers. I stay in touch with her by phone, though I would very much like to stand in the same sun as she is, watching her run or sharing a meal with her.

I wonder about the identity issues she will have to learn to live with, the attitude she will adopt in her daily life, and the narratives she will need as she navigates the tightrope of the post-genocide reality. As a parent, I hope I can be of some help to her in this regard, but I know she will have to figure it out for herself.

My dad still lives in Rwanda, where he serves the Evangelical Church to this day. We speak often. He prays for me over the phone now.

Joel also still lives in Rwanda. He teaches mathematics in a city high school and is married with two beautiful children, a girl and a boy.

Auntie Abayo went to university, where she did her undergraduate degree in business science. She is married and has five kids, four boys and a girl. She, too, lives in Rwanda, and works in the NGO sector.

Luc and Auntie Peace are also still there. Peace is quite a successful entrepreneur. She is married and has two kids. After working for a variety of different companies, Luc recently started his own small business buying, refurbishing, and selling second-hand furniture. He and his wife have four kids.

I love and miss them all. We went through a lot together.

ONE OF MY favourite thinkers is Saul of Tarsus, also known as Saint Paul. Just like Revelation, Paul's work is much debated and often misunderstood.

It was Paul who said, "And we know that in all things God works for the good of those who love Him, who have been called according to His purpose." Many have used these words to argue that God works for the good of Christians only, but I see it differently. If God is the ever-loving, ever-merciful Creator, then surely "those who have been called according to His purpose" are those who strive to be as loving and merciful as they can be. Paul is saying, simply, that when we love others, we align ourselves with God, and so aligned, whom shall we fear? It is in the common good, therefore, that we find our highest purpose.

At times I lose sight of this purpose and feel overwhelmed by the challenges and all the issues this world has to offer, but with prayer and daily practice I am able, mostly, to connect with it. And we carry on walking. All of us together.

I talk to that kid in the forest sometimes. I try to help him. I tell him that even if it is hard to believe, life will get better. Yes, there is desolation and pain, yes, there is blood, but it is not what you are seeing now that matters but what will come. You are not dead. And guess what, you are not supposed to die, not for a long time. These bodies you see, still and broken in rivers, valleys, and forests, their time had come. Yours has not yet, Obadiah.

I also know why you hate drinking water, I say to him. You don't want to drink it because a voice insists that every drop is polluted by blood. I tell him not to believe it. Water runs, I say. And as it runs it changes and is changed.

(Dar es Salaam, November 2020)

IT TAKES A VILLAGE

Have you ever realized how hard it is to express gratitude to everyone who blessed your life in singular ways? I wish I could hug you all.

Truly, words cannot express the depth and width of your amazing support throughout the years that has led to the story you so dearly wanted to be read by the entire world. This journey would not have succeeded without the unflinching and unwavering support of many friends, some of whom I already met, some I have yet to meet, across North America and Africa. As wisdom teaches us, reiterated by Bruce Walsh, it takes a whole village to raise a child. How I wish I could list everyone on this page.

First and foremost, I want to thank God for His grace and mercy that has sustained me throughout the whole process of reorganizing and writing my first memoir, as painful as it was, to recollect the bloody valleys of the shadow of death, the sleepless nights of agony, the slippery mountains, deep rivers, and jungles; our God who mercifully refused to let us be swallowed as happened to other refugees!

Second, I wish to express my sincere gratitude to my father, who, by his prayerful life, has taught me the power of hope when everything seems to be falling apart.

Third, I am indebted to Mr. Bruce Walsh for being an outstanding collaborator and mentor; his infectious love, his calls, the funds he sent me when my pockets ran dry during the toughest pandemic in recent history, and his guidance throughout the process kept me on track. Bruce knew when to reassure me, especially when the route got rough. He never got tired of giving me insights on how to improve my book, connecting me with the right people, and providing me with the needed tools to move faster with the manuscript. *Die Walking* would not have seen publication without your unwavering support.

Fourth, my two siblings, whose resilience has always intrigued me. Throughout this process, I heavily relied on them. For each painful recollection of thoughts, I could see tears flowing inward. If tears could grow a garden, theirs could grow a forest. Indeed, in my culture a man has felt enough if tears run to his stomach. May my siblings find the deepest expression of our collective memory that we joyfully agreed to share with the world.

Finally, *Die Walking* is a story of humanity, of a world facing its responsibility when evil rules. The memoir is a drop in the ocean, but worth the read. There cannot be a book that rightfully expresses the sleepless nights, rainy days, hunger, and torture — emotional and physical — that refugees and other people go through at the hands of their oppressors. However, many helped bring it about. Ms. Laurena Zondo — who birthed the first version of this memoir — for the sharp eye and for sharing in my pain; Geoffrey York, for a carefully written foreword; Leighton and Merilyn Smith, for their unflinching financial support; Joshua Greenspon and Maria Golikova, for the thorough editing; Alysia Shewchuk for her amazing cover; Tilman Lewis for the copyedit and Gemma Wain for the proofread; Darrel, Kerry, and Mike Palmer for the unwavering support; the entire team at House of Anansi; and the many many friends who may not find their names herein: your overwhelming help is forever cherished.

Thanks to everyone for expressing *Ubuntu* in ways beyond the obvious. May you find herein my deep-felt gratitude for your love and care, without which *Die Walking* would have never seen its day. Thank you, all.

OBADIAH M. is the pseudonym of a Rwandan author living in East Africa. He writes anonymously to protect himself and his family from those who would prevent him from sharing his story.